# SEARCHING FOR FRITZI

## CAROL BERGMAN

MEDIACS
NEW YORK

Printed in the United States of America by

Mediacs

309 East 87th St. #7G, New York, NY 10128


Design by Dale Voelker

Cover drawing and photos by Chloe Bergman

The portrait of Fritzi Burger on page 37 is reprinted
by permission of AP/Wide World Photos


First Edition, 1999

Library of Congress Catalog Card Number: 99-90737


ISBN 0-9673134-0-6

*for my maternal grandparents*
*Nanette Feldmahr Grätzer*
*February 30, 1877- Auschwitz, 194(?)*
*Berthold Grätzer*
*July 29, 1872- April 15, 1942*

*and for my great-uncle*
*Dr. Arnold Grätzer*
*April 19, 1884- Auschwitz, 194(?)*

You who harmed a simple man,
do not feel secure, for a poet remembers.

– Czeslaw Milosz


All memories are echoes: some whisper,
others roar, as this does.

– Grace Schulman

## Preface: A Journey Begins

My journey began in earnest in 1989. At the time, my mother was seventy-seven and I was forty-five. After a lifetime of silence on the subject of the Holocaust, I insisted that before it was too late, my mother and I should attempt recording an oral history. After many months of procrastination, she finally agreed.

We met on a Sunday in her home, just the two of us sitting at the kitchen table. The house was quiet; my stepfather was out playing golf. "No more excuses," I began, gently.

At first, my mother kept asking whether I was certain the tape recorder was working properly or if I had noticed the new bird feeder outside the window but she soon forgot where she was and told one story after another about her years as a child and young adult in Vienna. One of these stories was about Fritzi Burger, my mother's second cousin. Fritzi was a champion figure skater and, by the age of sixteen or so, was very well known throughout Europe. Later, she went on to become a silver medalist in the 1928 and 1932 Olympics finishing second behind her perennial arch-rival, Sonja Henie.

Everyone in Vienna followed Fritzi's career avidly, as they did all sports celebrities. But my mother had a special interest in Fritzi. They were only two years apart in age and they were related. My mother had pleasant memories of going ice skating with Fritzi at the Wien Eislaufverein, a famous outdoor rink, still in existence, in the center of the city. My mother skated mostly on weekends, sometimes with her mother – my grandmother, Nanette – who was a very fine ice dancer herself, and then, as she got older, with her friends. Fritzi was often there, too, though she also trained at a rink on the other side of the city.

It was an event when Fritzi turned up at the Eislaufverein and my mother took advantage of it. The two girls held hands and skated round and round the rink together. Others must have looked on enviously. Many commented that Fritzi and my mother looked like sisters, which tickled my mother — an only child — even more.

My mother's description of Fritzi made her seem much older and more worldly than anyone else in the family. Perhaps this was because Fritzi was a celebrity and my mother looked up to her. In truth, my mother only knew Fritzi from afar; they were never intimates and saw each other only occasionally at the ice rink or at family gatherings.

"Whatever happened to Fritzi?" I asked, shattering her reverie. What I meant was, had she survived the war or been killed in a camp? My mother didn't know and was reluctant to hypothesize. Fritzi existed unscathed in the remote and innocent past, untarnished by Hitler's genocide or the agony of the Diaspora. So, too, did many other members of my mother's family. It seemed important to my mother to keep them there. But my questions—unrelenting, like those of a persistent child—forced her to move on, beyond the innocent past, through the darkness of the Nazi era, and into the present time. That was, after all what we had agreed to do together, however difficult.

"Tell me what you do know," I suggested. "And we'll go on from there."

But my mother had difficulty moving on. Instead, she continued reminiscing about Fritzi. She remembered that Fritzi's father had been a twin and that he and his brother, Fritzi's uncle, were often Fritzi's chaperones at competitions. She couldn't remember Fritzi's mother at all, or picture her, or recall her name, although she thought it might be Sadie Feldmahr. Feldmahr was my grandmother Nanette's maiden name. She remembered Fritzi's engagement to a German bob sledder, an engagement that was abruptly and mysteriously terminated. And she recalled that Fritzi was already married by her early twenties, to a Japanese man, perhaps a diplomat, my mother thought.

Fritzi had ended her skating career sometime after the 1932 Olympics. She'd gone to live in London, returning to Vienna with a baby boy just before Hitler's annexation of Austria in the spring of 1938. My mother has visual memories of kimonos on display either in Fritzi's home or the home of another relative. They were wonderfully exotic, as was Fritzi and her handsome, Japanese husband. There, Fritzi's history, and the thread of my mother's memory, is broken.

My mother made no attempt to reconnect with Fritzi after the war; why should she when they had never been close. Now, more than fifty years later, she was thinking about her again. It was odd, wasn't it, she said, that she didn't know what had happened to Fritzi. Yet when I asked if she'd like to search for her, she was surprisingly lukewarm to the idea. She didn't know how she would feel if we found her, she explained, or what she would say to her if they ever spoke again.

I turned off the tape recorder and offered to make some tea. Fritzi's ghost hovered, resonating with loss and pain.

"I have a sense of something unspoken here," I said. "Something about Fritzi you know but cannot say, or something you know but cannot articulate."

I could see my mother's face, which has always been unusually supple and expressive, become a scowl.

"I don't know why you are so interested in Fritzi," she said impatiently. "She's not worth it."

"Her story sounds interesting to me," I said, puzzled by the abrupt shift in my mother's mood. Just moments before she couldn't stop talking about Fritzi.

"There's a lot about Vienna you don't understand," she said.

"Isn't that why we're having this conversation?," I asked.

"There's a lot that's not worth knowing," she said.

"Everything is worth knowing," I argued. "Even if it hurts."

My tenacity alarmed my mother. In the past, like other children of survivors, I had felt protective of my mother and accepted her evasions without question; now I was no longer willing to do so.

"I'm going to search for Fritzi," I told her. "I think she'll lead us where we need to go."

# PART I : NEW YORK

## CHAPTER 1: LETTERS

I began with an inquiry to the Japanese Ministry of Foreign Affairs. If Fritzi's husband had been a diplomat, perhaps they would know about her.

*Ministry of Foreign Affairs*
*Tokyo 100, Japan*          *October 19, 1989*

*Personnel Department:*

*Your consulate in New York suggested I write to you... I am trying to trace a cousin of mine who was married to a member of your Foreign Service before World War II. My intention is to write about her and my family's search for her.*

*Before she married, my cousin's name was Fritzi Burger. She was an Austrian citizen and a well known international ice skating champion. She skated in the 1932 Olympics in Lake Placid, N.Y.*

*I do not know her husband's name but I do know that he was posted to London before the war. After that, my family lost track of Fritzi's movements. As an Austrian citizen married to a Japanese national, both she and her husband might have been interned in the U.K. or they might have had diplomatic immunity and returned to Japan. I also know that they had a child.*

*If you can be of any assistance in helping me trace Fritzi Burger and her family, it would of course be deeply appreciated.*

*Sincerely yours,*
*Carol Bergman*

*****

OOC *(Austrian Olympic Committee)*
A-1040 Vienna                          March 27, 1990

*Dear Sir/Madam,*

*Your consulate in New York suggested I write to you. I am a journalist based in New York… I am trying to trace a cousin of mine…*

*Sincerely yours,*
*Carol Bergman*

*****

"So, you wrote letters," my mother said. "Has there been any response?"

"No response," I said.

"Do you expect a response?"

"I have no expectation," I said.

Yet, with just the few desultory letters I wrote, Fritzi surfaced.

*****

*Graz, 8 February 1992*

*Dear Mrs. Bergman,*

*In March 1991 you have addressed a letter to the Austrian Olympic Committee with respect for help in searching the home address of your cousin Fritzi Burger who won in 1928 and 1932 two Olympic silver medals in figure skating. The OOC has sent me a copy of your letter hoping that I would be able as old Olympic historian to find a trace of Fritzi Burger. With great delay I have now succeeded with help of an old journalist friend in Vienna to find the needed trace.*

*Mrs. Frederika Russell, born Fritzi Burger, is now for vacances (skiing) in Austria.*

*Badgastein, Hotel Wildbad (region Salzburg)*
*Phone No. 06434/37-610*

*I am glad to be able to arrange the contact with your cousin and I would be very interested to receive a copy of your "Fritzi"- Frederika Burger-Russell -family story.*

*With all good wishes for your work and kind regards*


*Yours sincerely*
*Erich Kamper*
*Olympic Historian*
*Holder of the Olympic order*
*honorary member of the International Olympic Academy*
*Athens/Olympia*


*****

Graz, 6 March 1992

*To the editor office with the request to send this letter to:*
*Mrs. Carol Bergman (journalist) Christian Science Monitor*
*Wooster, Oh 44691/USA*
*Dear Mrs. Bergman,*

*As you see my letter of 8 February has been returned because of inxact address. It's a bad photocopy which I received from the Austrian Olympic Committee in Vienna of your letter of 27 March, 1990.*

*Meanwhile I had a contact by letter with Mrs. Russell, nee Fritzi Burger, who spent her skiing holidays in Badgastein. To my great surprise Mrs. Russell informed me that she has no cousin and that she has never heard yet your name. The brothers and sisters of her parents had no children according to the message of Mrs. Russell. In which relations should be your family to Friederike "Fritzi" Burger? Perhaps it's an error!*

*Mrs. Russell has for principle reasons refused to give me her home address in the USA. Perhaps you have a chance to learn her home address in the office of the Hotel Wildbad A-5640 Badgastein (region Salzburg), phone no. 06434/3761, teleprinter 67523 (Wilda).*

*May I confess that your problem is rather mysterious for me, but I had the intention to help you in your researches.*

*With kind regards*

*Yours sincerely,*
*Erich Kamper*
*enclosed: returned letter*

\*\*\*\*\*

*Fritzi Burger Russell*
*c/o Hotel Wildbad*
*A-5640 Badgastein*
*Austria*

*April 17, 1992*

Dear Mrs. Russell,

I am writing to you on behalf of my mother, Gerda Grätzer Poll, who has fond memories of skating with you when she was a child. Her mother, (my grandmother), Nina (Nanette) Feldmahr was related to your mother.

Your name came up as I was doing an oral history with my mother. She wondered how you had fared over the years. I offered to use my journalistic expertise to attempt to trace you. I wrote to the Olympic Committee, and they passed my letter on to Mr. Erich Kamper, the Olympic historian, who lives in Graz. He was puzzled because, of course, my name—Bergman—would mean nothing to you.

My mother is now eighty years old. I believe you are about the same age. Enclosed, her address should you feel inclined to write to her directly. I know it would mean a lot to her to hear from you.

Sincerely yours,
Carol Bergman

*****

Erich Kamper
A-8010 Graz
Austria

April 27, 1992

Dear Mr. Kamper,

Many thanks for your two letters (8 February and 6 March) which
were forwarded to me by The Christian Science Monitor…
I appreciate your efforts and look forward to hearing from you again
should you contact Mrs. Burger-Russell. Also, if you would like information regarding Mrs. Burger-Russell's early years, I am sure my
mother would oblige with a few reminiscences…

Sincerely yours,
Carol Bergman

I called my mother. "Fritzi has an address in America," I said.
She's on a skiing holiday in Austria. I have the  phone number of
the hotel. Do you want to call her?"

There was a long pause before she said, "You've found Fritzi?
It's not possible."

"Yes.  She's alive. But she says she has no cousins."

"I told you she wasn't worth it. Why should I bother calling
her? Forget it."

Once again, my mother was resisting my efforts with
incredulity and anger. She wanted me to stop; she made this clear.
But, by now, Fritzi  had settled in my imagination and was resting
on my shoulder, still formless, a spirit memory. Who was she to me

and why was I becoming obsessed with her? A distant cousin? A famous figure skater? Or more?

I thought of my mother's words again: She's not worth it.

What did she mean? Maybe that any effort to retrieve the past was "not worth it" because the memories caused too much pain.

There was some resistance in me, too, though I didn't want to admit it at the time. I didn't want to hurt my mother. How could I press on without her blessing and cooperation?

Night after night in a tormented restless sleep, I dreamt of Fritzi. She was faceless, without a body, without history, an emblem of everything I, too, had lost in the Holocaust. What sorrows would be unleashed if I kept going?

## CHAPTER 2: WHY FRITZI?

Time passed. I dreamt of suitcases, one dream after another. Packing, unpacking. Old leather valises with brass fittings containing priceless personal possessions, all left behind. My cousin, George, also the child of survivors, tells me he has the same dreams, a continuing motif.

"Do you ever retrieve the lost case?" I asked him once.

"Never," he said. "Occasionally variations on a theme, but the cases are always lost, misplaced, or forgotten."

"Are they ever stolen?"

"No, not stolen. Lost."

"Mine too," I said.

*****

"Why Fritzi?," my neighbor, Isaak Arbus, wanted to know, reiterating the question I had already been asking myself, in my waking hours, in my dreams. Was it because Fritzi was a celebrity that I was so interested in her? Why was it so important to me to claim her as "family?"

It was a warm spring day, the roses in front of our building in full bloom, the red and yellow tulips swaying in a light breeze. Isaak, a survivor of twelve camps, was wearing a short- sleeved shirt. Clearly visible were the  letters his Nazi keepers had carved into his arm. Standing there talking to him on that warm spring day, all I had vaguely felt or half understood about my growing obsession with Fritzi came into sharp focus, then drifted again into mist.

"Most of my family was murdered in the camps," I said.

The word "murdered," sat at attention between us. When I was young, only euphemisms such as "perished" were permitted.

Isaak didn't flinch. "And?" he said, pushing me further.

"And we found Fritzi," I said, tentatively, still not understanding the significance of Fritzi's denial of her connection to my family in this unfolding story.

I remember feeling shocked when my mother first revealed to me that her mother, my grandmother, Nanette, was the youngest of ten siblings. My mother's childhood years, though she was an only child, were filled with aunts and uncles and cousins in abundance. A cornucopia of attachments. They were all wiped out, like a teacher taking an eraser to a blackboard, in Hitler's Final Solution.

Often, when I was growing up, despite affluence, I felt as though the earth under my feet was limpid, like a water bed, and that my family had nothing to fall back on in times of stress and strife except themselves and their own fortitude.

All my friends had relatives, but I did not. Grandparents where they spent Sunday afternoons and holidays. Grandparents who gave them toys and took them on vacation. In their homes there were photographs cascading off the mantel piece or piano in ornate decorative frames and family stories that went with the photographs about an eccentric aunt or a picnic that took place at the turn of the century. Heirlooms, dowries, hand-me-downs. My sister and I had none of this. Everything in our home—the furniture, the appliances, the clothes we wore—was modern in feel and design, enviable because it was cutting-edge, but without history.

Friends were around, other refugees, with attenuated or newly constituted families of their own. We relied on each other, adopted each other, cared for each other, and we got together often, but it wasn't the same as having extended family in attendance, as having a clan. Oddly, religion never came into it, rarely was discussed. We were Jews, but what did that mean? We went to synagogue from time to time, the boys were Bar Mitzvahed, we lit the candles during Chanukah and sang songs. I wanted a Christmas tree like all my friends, and was told "No," but without much explanation. I felt different but not desperately enough to worry about it. I was an American and in America everyone came from somewhere else.

But this still didn't explain why I had no family. As a child, I never knew, never asked, never was told. Everyone had "perished," and this piece of titillating information was voiced quietly, a mere whisper, a hush. When would I be considered old enough to tolerate the truth? Probably never.

Eventually, I read <u>The Diary of Anne Frank</u> and began to figure things out for myself using my own words: I was a member of a persecuted remnant band, a child of survivors.

I learned there were others like us, scattered here, scattered there. Two cousins in Los Angeles, another in Australia, one in Israel, one in Austria. Everyone accounted for, more or less. Until Fritzi.

*****

During the run-up to the Olympics in late January, 1994, Fritzi surfaced again. A sports reporter from The New York Times tracked her down in Maine, where, it turned out, Fritzi had lived since 1969. The reporter wanted to know what Fritzi thought of the Tonya Harding-Nancy Kerrigan affair and whether such jealousies and scandals happened when she was a young skater in the 1920's.

I read the article with excitement hoping there would be some personal information about Fritzi and her family, but there was none.

## CHAPTER 3: DENIAL

I telephoned my mother. "There's a profile of Fritzi in the newspaper," I said. "It's in the sports pages. You might have missed it."

"I never read the sports pages. Why should I read the sports pages?"

"Don't be angry with me. I want you to call her."

"I won't call."

"She's living in Maine. Give me an hour, I'll get the number."

I had already contacted Maine information and learned the number was unlisted but I didn't tell my mother this. I wanted to give her a chance to say she'd changed her mind, that Fritzi was "worth it," and that she wanted to speak to her.

"What will I say?"

"You'll think of something."

I got off the phone and put on my journalist's hat. If a phone number is unlisted, first line of defense is to call City Hall and ask for the person in charge of the voter registration rolls. Within fifteen minutes, I had the number. Did I tell the woman who answered the phone that Fritzi was a relative? No, I did not. I told her I was a journalist on a story. This was not a lie nor was it entirely the truth. I didn't care. I was feeling wired. Fritzi was real, she was alive. I couldn't wait to talk to her, to throw my arms around her, to introduce her to my daughter, Chloe. I fantasized a family reunion with my sister and her children, our husbands, at a long table overflowing with food and memories.

I telephoned my mother again. "I've got the number, " I said.

"Do you want to call or should I?"

"I'll call," she said.

I waited by the phone, tried to keep busy, boiled a kettle for tea. More than a half hour passed.

"I can't believe it. It's what I had feared. Fritzi says she doesn't remember me," my mother said.

She wasn't hurt, she was mad. I, however, was stunned. Not because of Fritzi's strange memory loss, but because of my mother's word "fear."

My mother is tough, driven, prescient, direct, and, also, dissembling. Her deepest feelings are unknown to me, embedded at times in seemingly irrational statements and erratic behavior. To understand her, I have had to learn to break her codes. On the subject of her reluctance to talk to Fritzi, she never revealed to me exactly what she feared when I began the search. I made assumptions, intuited theories. Now that I had found Fritzi, I had another hypothesis: my mother was afraid Fritzi would choose not to remember her. She was afraid that by not remembering her, or pretending not to remember her, Fritzi would obliterate the memory of our family, threadbare, like old lace, after so many years. This was too much to bear.

"She says we couldn't be cousins. Her mother was Marie Kopp, a Catholic from Hungary, not Sadie Feldmahr. I didn't even ask if she was Jewish, yet she said, 'I'm not Jewish.'"

"But what does this mean?" I asked.

It hadn't occurred to me that Fritzi might not be Jewish or might be only half Jewish or a quarter Jewish. From my vantage point in America in the 1990's, to even voice these distinctions felt wrong to me. But in Austria, when my mother and Fritzi were growing up, antisemitism was endemic and ruthless and these distinctions were important to Jews and Christians, citizens and *Ausländer*.[1] Before Hitler, conversion was a viable solution for many. Between 1891 and 1914, 12,000 Viennese Jews converted to Christianity, mostly young men who wanted to marry Christian women or academics who wanted to teach at the University. It was the highest conversion rate in all of Europe. Between 1919 and 1937, as Nazism gained power, there were 17,000 defections from the Jewish community, either conversions or registration as *Konfessionslos*, without religion.

"It would have been difficult for Fritzi to skate competitively if she'd been a Jew," my mother said, brusquely.

I had done some reading and knew this was true. Even before Hitler, since the early 1920's, many sports clubs in Germany and Austria were "Aryanized." Some Jewish athletes set up clubs of their own, others converted and joined the Aryan clubs. For at least a decade before Hitler came to power, antisemitic "volkist" notions pervaded sports in both countries, culminating in the celebration of Nazi racist ideology at the 1936 Winter Olympic Games in Garmisch-Partenkirchen, Germany, and the Summer Olympic games that same year in Berlin. At the winter games, there were Jews representing other countries and the Nazis even

---

1. I have chosen to spell antisemitism using only lower case letters and without hyphenation following Robert Wistrich's example in his book, <u>Antisemitism; The Longest Hatred.</u> Like Wistrich, I believe the word "Semite" to be a Nazi construct to define an imaginary "race." "Semite" refers to a group of people who speak related "Semitic" languages. I have not changed the spelling inside other peoples' quotes.

invited Helene Mayer, originally from Offenbach, to compete even though she had emigrated to the United States. They rationalized this bizarre invitation with an explanation: Mayer was Jewish but she had two "Aryan" grandparents.

My mother continued.

"I'm all confused. I thought her father wasn't Jewish but now she says her mother wasn't either. I've never seen denial like this before. It's an affront to the family, to everyone who was killed."

This was clear. No more hypothesizing was necessary. I felt relieved.

"What about Hedy Haslinger?" I asked. "Didn't she marry a Catholic?"

Both Hedy, my mother's cousin, and her daughter, Dorrith, survived the war in Vienna, camouflaged by their Catholicism. But they were lucky the Nazis didn't find them because Hitler, ultimately, made no distinctions.

"Hedy and Dorrith have never denied their origins or rejected our family," my mother explained. "They never said, like Fritzi said, 'It's not possible. I can't be your cousin.' I know who Fritzi is. She is my cousin. She was shocked when I asked whether her father was a twin. How did I know? Because I'm her cousin, that's how I know."

My mother was angry. Fritzi was polite. In between the more difficult moments, the two women reminisced about Vienna where Fritzi still traveled at least once a year. And after a while she said, "I do remember ice skating with a Gerda Grushner. Was that you?"

"My maiden name was Grätzer," my mother said, impatiently.

"But the person you remember could have been me."

At times, my mother admitted she was disarmed by Fritzi's graciousness. But I suspected that Fritzi had a public persona and was good at this. My mother could have been anyone—a stranger, a fan, an acolyte, someone from before the war who remembered Fritzi in her prime as a world famous figure skater.

They spoke in German and they did talk personally, my mother said. They were both widows living alone. Both had been married twice, both were still active, though Fritzi, extraordinary at the age of 83, still skied, played tennis and swam. My mother had given up skiing and tennis many years ago and had two hip replacements, but she still swam, gardened, played bridge, belonged to two book clubs. Only my mother knew how much she resembled Fritzi, because she had seen Fritzi's photograph in the newspaper. "We look alike," she told her. But my hair is permed and I have green eyes. I remember your eyes are blue," my mother said, more kindly.

Then she asked if Fritzi would mind speaking to me. I was a writer and eager to ask her some questions.

*****

I looked at the photograph of Fritzi again in the newspaper, sipped my tea. It was uncanny how much Fritzi looked like my mother and like another cousin, Lily, whose photograph I had seen some years ago for the first time. And I could see myself in Fritzi's face—high cheekbones, square jaw—like my grandmother Nanette. Behind Fritzi's impish smile, I thought I saw pride, tenacity, and melancholy held at bay, all attributes familiar to children of survivors. But <u>was</u> Fritzi a survivor? I wasn't sure.

The photographer had seated Fritzi in front of a bookcase, an emblem of culture and education. In what way would her living room mirror my mother's which was also overflowing with books, paintings and artifacts? Did Fritzi, too, have a piano? And what about her children and grandchildren? "She has a son by her second marriage," my mother had said. "But I don't know where he is or what happened to the baby she brought back to Vienna."

How to begin? Fritzi told my mother she was not a cousin and she was not Jewish. I tried to write down a few questions with this in mind but I felt dead-ended.

Nothing to do but to dial the number. And talk.

"Yes. Your mother told me you were going to call," Fritzi began, warmly. Her voice was lighter than my mother's and not as heavily accented because, I remembered, she'd lived in London and learned English there.

"There's something mysterious happening here," I began. "My mother is sure you are cousins, related through your mothers, but you say your mother was Marie Kopp."

Then, quickly, though I hadn't asked about their religious affiliations, she added, "My father was Protestant. My mother was Catholic. Her family were military people. The old Austro-Hungarian Empire."

She sounded so sure that I began to doubt my mother's memory. Then I thought again of the photograph; the family resemblance was palpable.

Fritzi had told Erich Kamper, the Olympic historian, that there were no cousins on either side of her family. Did she really believe this? Was she lying? Or was the memory of her Jewish origins a suppressed memory only accessible through hypnosis like childhood incest?

"Oh well, I suppose it doesn't matter if we are related or not," she said, finally. "Come up and see me when I get back from Europe in March."

Again, graciousness, even warmth. I couldn't figure it out.

I thought that was the end of our conversation, but Fritzi wanted to talk more. I listened attentively as she began spinning out part of her life story, which she did easily and without much prompting from me.

"Do you still ice skate?" I asked.

"Not for a long time," she said. "I gave it up. Never give up something you love," she said, ruefully.

I wondered if she had given it up for love, or for other reasons. She was always coming in second behind Sonja Henie, her own career eclipsed by Henie's fame. This must have been a frustration. And then there was the question of her Jewish ancestry. What would have happened to Fritzi if it had been exposed?

Fritzi attended the Winter Games in 1936 as an observer, she told me, but by then she was already married and retired from competitive sport. Henie was there, too, but as a competitor. She won yet another gold medal. A photograph, splattered all over the world press at the time, shows Henie curtsying to Hitler. At an exhibition prior to the Olympics, she'd been observed giving the Nazi salute. She had even dined with Hitler at Berchtesgarden and accepted an autographed photograph of him.

And there was antisemitism in America, too. At Lake Placid,

New York, where Fritzi skated four years earlier in the 1932 Winter Olympics, there was a scandal before the games began. The Lake Placid Club had always been restricted to members of the "Gentile persuasion," according to the Club's bye-laws, which read in part: "From its foundation the invariable rule has been to admit no Hebrews." It was therefore unconscionable, wrote David N. Mosessohn, Chairman of the National Council of The Jewish Tribune to Franklin Delano Roosevelt, Governor of New York, for the State of New York to allocate $60,000 of taxpayer money, some of it Jewish taxpayer money, to build a new bobsled run, new roads, and a new stadium to benefit a private, restricted club after the games were over.

The debate continued for more than a month and was reported assiduously in The New York Times. Finally, it was resolved. The solution: a decision to deed the bobsled run, the new stadium, the roads, to the township rather than the Club. FDR's reputation was spared, the Jewish protest was stilled, the games would go on.

"Do you remember skating at Lake Placid?," I asked.

"Lake Placid was beautiful," she said. "I won a silver there, too, you know."

"In 1932. Yes, I know," I said.

I knew about the incident too, but didn't mention it to Fritzi. What would be the point? She wasn't Jewish, right? And, therefore, she could have stayed anywhere in Lake Placid even though it was known that most hotels and lodges and inns in the vicinity of the resort were also restricted and remained restricted until the early 1960's.

Fritzi wasn't Jewish. The restriction didn't affect her. How fortunate, I thought.

Her first husband was a Japanese businessman not a diplomat as my mother had remembered. He was a Mikimoto, a wealthy family in Japan, internationally known for their cultured pearls. And they did have a son, Yoshi, born in 1937 during a return trip to Vienna after a four year sojourn in London.

"My mother remembers, Yoshi," I said. "And kimonos. Did you bring gifts?"

"I don't remember," Fritzi said. The brightness in her voice was fading. I had mentioned my mother's memory and she had not denied this memory. Maybe we were getting somewhere?

"When did your parents die?" I asked, startling even myself with the directness of the question. If one of her parents had been Jewish or even a converted Jew, perhaps he or she had died in a camp. Or perhaps Fritzi didn't know or did know and didn't want to remember?

Fritzi answered too quickly, I thought, and her answer didn't make much sense.

"They both died when they were fifty," she said. "My father in 1930 and my mother..." And now she hesitated creating an ellipsis in what had been, thus far, a free flow of sentences. "She died in 1938. Yes. It was 1938."

The year Hitler marched into Vienna.

"Of a heart attack," she continued. "I myself had a heart attack six years ago."

"And you are well, now?" I asked, worrying, selfishly, that Fritzi might die before a meeting could take place. I was also trying to process the coincidence of both her parents dying at age fifty.

Possible, but unlikely, I thought, the mystery of Fritzi's history deepening.

"Oh yes, very well," she said. "Yoshi would like me to move out West to live with him."

Why had I assumed Yoshi was dead? Maybe it was something my mother had said.

"Yoshi is your only child?"

"I have stepchildren from my second marriage and grandchildren, too. But Yoshi is my only one. He grew up in Japan. We lived there for thirty years until we came to the States with my second husband, Mr. Russell, in 1969. I met him when he was in Tokyo working for Citibank."

"You were there throughout the war?"

"Why yes, of course."

"And you speak Japanese?"

"Why yes, of course,"

I was feeling overwhelmed again. It was the revelation that I had a Japanese cousin and that he was living in America.

"Yoshi finished his education here," she said. "He builds houses."

"Houses?"

"Yes. He used to work in Japan a lot. But now he works mostly here. He's living in a small town in Washington up near the Canadian border."

By now, I was furiously taking notes and making plans to track Yoshi down. How could I justify asking Fritzi for his number? Or his last name?

"Would you like my phone number?" I asked as our conversation was winding down. "Did my mother give you hers?"

"Why don't you call me again in March," she said, almost dismissively.

Her disinterest in taking my phone number concerned me. I worried that she might change her mind about her invitation that we get together when she returned from Europe. I worried I would never meet Yoshi, my Japanese cousin.

*****

"She's invited us up to Maine," I told my mother. "What do you think? Shall we go?"

"She doesn't know who I am."

"When she sees you she'll know."

"Let's go," she said.

## CHAPTER 4: PROOF

Fritzi was traveling to Europe. She felt at home there and went back every year she told me. She would be in Vienna during the 1994 winter Olympics in Lillehammer. Her plan was to watch the skating from her hotel room and then go up to the mountains to ski.

I had a plan, too: I wanted to find Yoshi. I tried for days without success. My phone bill soared. And I was beginning to feel uncomfortable with my deception. I had become a spy, a guerrilla fighter, Fritzi and her denial the enemy. What had stopped me from calling Fritzi back and simply asking her for Yoshi's phone number?

I went to the library to begin my research. I was telling everyone I knew about Fritzi including a cousin of my husband's who is a retired librarian.

"If you are still looking for evidence about the Jewish background of Fritzi, I suggest that the easy way is to look at col. 1376 of v. 12 of the Encyclopedia Judaica," he wrote in a cryptic note.

In mid-March, I headed for the Jewish Division, Room 84, at the New York Public Library and found Fritzi's name clearly listed among other notable Jewish Olympians in the Encyclopedia Judaica. I took down the name of the author of the particular article. With a journalist's healthy skepticism, I wondered how the information had been compiled. What was the author's source? Skepticism aside, however, to see Fritzi's name included on that list gave me a perverse sense of satisfaction. That night I called my mother, I called Chloe, I called friends. I now had "proof" that

Fritzi had lied.

But the next morning, I felt more confused. The list was certainly not definitive. And why was I trying so hard to prove that Fritzi had a Jewish father or mother? Maybe it was because she was so adamant that she wasn't Jewish and wasn't related to us. I couldn't have cared less about the Jewish part; it was the rejection of us as family that hurt. Unfortunately, it seemed, one was contingent on the other. Or, conversely, if Fritzi admitted she was related to us, she would also be admitting her Jewish background. Either way, Fritzi was overly-aware of the stigma of being Jewish, a state-of-mind Cambridge University Professor Steven Beller calls "negative consciousness."

"Indeed, any contemporary denial will in itself be evidence of at least a negative consciousness," writes Beller in his book, Vienna and the Jews 1867-1938. "The background to this is that Vienna was the major centre of anti-Semitism in Europe before WWI and the only capital city at that time to have elected an anti-Semitic government. In other words, it was impossible to ignore the Jewish problem-affirmation and denial were two sides of the same coin."

So, where do we go from here I asked myself day after day, feeling lost and unsure where my journey was taking me. I telephoned my mother. "Let's at least touch base with Fritzi," I suggested, still hoping we could make a trip to Maine. The happy reunion fantasies would not abate.

On April 10, 1994 my mother called Fritzi for the second time. In that conversation, she told Fritzi she was taking her granddaughter to Vienna in June and would therefore have to postpone our reunion until the summer. This suited Fritzi better, too, as she had broken her arm while she was on her skiing holiday and needed time to heal. Fritzi reiterated again that it wasn't possible we were related and she certainly wasn't Jewish, although, again, my mother didn't ask.

Then a letter arrived from Franzi Klug, another cousin, living in Israel. Of course she remembered Fritzi, didn't everyone? And she remembered the family connection, too. Fritzi's grandmother and my mother's grandmother were sisters, both born "Steiners." My mother had gotten the Feldmahr connection wrong. Sadie Feldmahr was not Fritzi's mother after all, but the essence of the relationship as remembered by my mother, was correct; they were second cousins.

I sat down to write another letter to Fritzi:

*April 12, 1994*

*Dear Fritzi,*

*My mother, Gerda Poll, tells me she spoke with you on the telephone the other day. I was sorry to hear about your skiing injury and hope you are healing well and not in any discomfort. We look forward to coming up to see you in the summer which seems to be a better time for all of us.*

*I think some of the mystery about our family relationship has been cleared up. My mother received a letter from another cousin, Franzi, who remembers that my mother's grandmother and your maternal grandmother were sisters. Memory often confuses us and my mother had gotten some of the facts of your relationship wrong.*

*I believe your maternal grandmother's maiden name was "Steiner." She married a Kopp (correct spelling?) and your mother's maiden name was Kopp. Your mother than married Mr. Burger. Am I correct so far? On my mother's side, her maternal grandmother's maiden name was also "Steiner" and she was your grandmother's sister. My mother's grandmother married a Feldmahr. My mother's mother was a Feldmahr and she married Berthold Grätzer, my mother's father.*

*And so we have it. Your mother and my mother's mother were first cousins. You and my mother are second cousins.*

*Fritzi, I don't know what else to say about all this except that we are delighted to have found you and look forward to meeting you. I calculate that Yoshi is about my age (I just turned fifty) and that he is my third cousin, or second cousin twice removed, or whatever. I would love to talk to him.*

*I look forward to hearing your comments about our family tree and to talking with you in person sometime in July.*

*Best regards,*
*Carol Bergman*

I drew a hypothetical family tree in two configurations — one describing the family connection through Fritzi's father, the other through her mother, and enclosed it with the letter.

On Friday, April 22, 1994, my mother came into Manhattan for the day. My plan was to take her to the library to scan some of the Austrian newspapers on microfiche. I cannot read German and needed her to be my translator.

I was looking for a profile of Fritzi that might contain some personal information about her family life, perhaps even mention her mother and father. We pulled film of the Neue Freie Presse from 1926 to 1928 and set to work. This was the newspaper my mother had read when she lived in Vienna and to see it again was unsettling for her. I could feel her trembling. She recognized the bylines of various journalists and knew precisely who was a Nazi and who was not. She began to mumble angry words about Fritzi. "She's not worth it," she said over and over again. "Why are we doing this?"

There was very little information about any sports figures in this newspaper. Most columns were devoted to politics and economics. Human interest stories focused on suicides and murders. Vienna, then and now, has one of the highest suicide and child abuse rates in the world.

Fritzi's name appeared on several occasions within a report of a skating event, at world competitions, and then at the 1928 winter Olympics in St. Moritz where she won her first silver medal. But that was all. It was disappointing.

A day later, a letter arrived, handwritten on blue stationery:

*April 19, 1994*

*Dear Mrs. Bergman,*

*I have received your letter of April 12, 1994. I don't know any of the names in that letter with the exception of my mother's maiden name. How you got her name is puzzling to me. Apparently somebody had called a former skater who in turn called me when I was on the Arlberg* and asked for my mother's maiden name. It's a peculiar way of getting an information. If you want any information write to me or my lawyer with whom I have discussed the matter and who is fully informed, do not telephone. And do not call any of former skaters. I do not want you to write about me and I do not give interviews. I am cancelling the invitation to come and see me.

Fritzi Russell


April 24, 1994

Dear Fritzi,

I am very saddened by your letter of April 19. I had no intention of distressing you with revelations of family connections which I think, Fritzi, at this point are undeniable. Of course we will not come up to see you if you do not wish it. What would be the point?

As for how I discovered your mother's maiden name, you will recall that you gave my mother that information yourself during your first telephone conversation with her on January 28, 1994, the day an interview with you appeared in The New York Times.

I will not telephone you again though I will take you up on your offer to write to you with any further questions I might have.

Sincerely yours,
Carol Bergman


My mother sat down to write a letter to Fritzi, too, though she didn't tell me she had done so until a least a week later. She kept no copy and wrote it by hand expressing regret that Fritzi had taken our efforts to establish contact with her so badly. And she included a photograph my sister had taken of her after the interview with Fritzi had appeared in The New York Times in which my mother is seated in her wood-paneled office and is wearing a turtle neck sweater, just like Fritzi.

"She'll see the picture and she'll know," my mother said.

But we both agreed we would probably never hear from Fritzi Burger again.

\*\*\*\*\*

It was becoming obvious to me that I had to go to Vienna again with my mother. The encounter with Fritzi had been a troubling one, raising more questions for me than it answered, initiating a journey I could not abandon easily. It seemed logical that the next phase should be in Vienna.

I'd been there once before, in the summer of 1973, but my recollections of that trip were insignificant, or perhaps I wasn't ready, at that stage of my life, to ask questions or to hear the answers, assuming my mother might have been prepared to break her silence at that time. Except for one or two puzzling encounters, it was a casual visit accomplished in a matter of days and then it was over, and nearly forgotten.

I was now in a different phase of my life—middle age, between the past as symbolized by my mother, and the future as symbolized by my daughter. Literally, a link between two generations, and the experience of the Holocaust.

My mother and Chloe had been planning a trip for some time, even before Fritzi surfaced. They graciously agreed I could tag along.

As departure neared, my mother became more and more anxious. The apprehension became somatic, affecting her bones and joints. At night, she awoke unable to swallow, mentally packing her bags, worrying that she would leave everything important behind. In these dreams, so similar to my own, she found herself walking along the cobblestoned streets of her youth, the only audible sound that of her teeth rattling.

In the daylight hours, her fear became more concrete. The war raging in the former Yugoslavia could spill over into the rest of Europe while we were traveling. It was only a matter of kilometers. The NATO aircraft would be crisscrossing the skies. What if while we were there, the borders were sealed and we would be unable to return home?

Chloe was the only one who could calm my mother down.

"It's all right Baba. I'll be there," she said.

"I'm only going for you," my mother told her.

I thought, angrily, of Fritzi moving in and out of Vienna year after year with ease, unencumbered, apparently, with memory, unfazed by the knowledge that a city once blessed with 200,000 Jews was now almost entirely ethnically cleansed.[2] Jews scattered in the Diaspora. Jews murdered in the camps. Members of Fritzi's own family among them, yet she didn't seem to know or care.

---

2. There are now about 6,000 Jews living in Vienna, 8,000 in Austria.

*My grandparents on their wedding day, 1905.*

*My mother, Gerda Grätzer Poll
in her study, January 1994.*

*Photo of Fritzi published in
The New York Times, January 28, 1994.*
*(AP/Wide World Photos)*

Mrs. Slunsky and her daughter, Johanna,
in front of the Haslinger Glove Store.

My mother, revisiting the
university, summer 1994.

Chloe and me in front
of Josefinefasse #4.

My mother, cousin Dorrith, and Chloe.
I am on the far left.

*Our cousin, Dorrith, in the center.*

*Working up the courage to knock on the door of my mother's childhood home.*

*My mother standing on her father's burial mound.*

*The stone we erected on Berthold's grave. Nanette is also mentioned on the stone though her ashes are in Auschwitz.*

*My mother and other visitors at the gate of the Little Fort in Theresienstadt.*

*My mother contemplating the Monument Against War & Fascism
in central Vienna. The Old Jew is in the background.*

# PART II: VIENNA

## CHAPTER 5: DEUTSCH

The first shock is hearing my mother speak German again. The second, that I understand nearly everything. Within days of our arrival in Vienna on June 7, 1994, I am dreaming in German and sounding like a Viennese. Ja Ja, with a strange dismissive shake of the head. But in my waking hours, I cannot speak German. My 20-year-old daughter, Chloe, a second-generation American, finds this fascinating; I am alarmed. Why does this language feel so comfortable to me?

I try to explain, to myself, to others. How is it I can understand but not speak? Is it because, like an elective mute, I choose not to speak?

I grew up in a household of refugees who spoke in a language I did not share. During World War II, German was the language of the enemy and my parents thought it wise not to speak German on the streets of New York City. At home they made a concerted effort to speak German only to each other and English to their American offspring. My sister and I were given the most American names imaginable. Carol Ann. Joan Frances. I never heard stories told in German or saw it written down. When I watched my parents and their friends speak to one another, it was as though I was watching deaf people miming in sign language. I made up stories to go with gestures. Mouths opened and the voice inside me spoke, like an actor dubbing the words into a cartoon face. I was alone in this world observing it from the outside in.

Eventually, I learned to decode German but have no conscious recollection of when this ability became solidified. The secrets that were now mine were terrifying. Somewhere inside the mysterious grammar of my parents' mother tongue was betrayal. A language of belonging, but not belonging. A language that was theirs, but not theirs. Certainly, it was not mine. Or so I thought.

Every day during our stay in Vienna there are misunderstandings. My mother is somewhat hard of hearing, refusing to wear an aid, and she will often answer a question or comment with a non sequitur. The concierge at the hotel inquires if she'd like a newspaper. She answers, yes, she's had a fine day. The waiter asks if she'd like some water. She says yes, some more bread would be wonderful. I find myself correcting her reply, or re-translating the question for her into English.

There is a barrier my mother will not cross, into the broad dialect of the underclass. She was raised an educated, cultured Viennese, her idiom and diphthongs mirroring Schönbrunnerdeutsch, the German spoken by the Hapsburgs, until the end of World War I, Austro-Hungary's benevolent monarchs. Their German (named after Schönbrunn Castle) was adopted by the aristocrats, the students at the university, doctors  lawyers, professionals, secular Jews. That "other" language was for the urban working class, the rural peasants, and the underground Nazis. Later it became the language of Hitler's Reich. Hitler was an Austrian from Linz, his language more vulgar, more percussive, more guttural, than anyone had ever heard before. This is now the language of the Viennese.

Some say that Viennese dialect as it is spoken today is a language signifying the democratization of the culture. The language of the young, of popular culture, is more vernacular and universal.

Nearly all the Jews of my mother's generation are gone. Who are the Viennese intelligentsia now and what language do they speak?

"Even the educated Viennese speak in dialect," my mother says. "But I cannot answer in dialect. It is impossible. If I could leave tomorrow, I would leave."

The ambiance of the language frightens me, too, triggering a learned helplessness. Maybe this is why I cannot speak. I envision scenes from the past as I have been reading about them in books, or seen them on film, and they are clouding my ability to process what is happening in the present. My mother, however, has real memories from the past to suppress or transcend. Is this friendly young man instructing us about how to obtain tickets for the Opera an underground Nazi?

"Baba what are you talking about," Chloe asks. "He's a student just like me. Didn't you notice him studying when we came in late last night?"

"That doesn't mean he's not a Nazi," my mother says.

It is wartime again. Nazis on every corner, in every shop, behind the concierge's desk at the hotel. When does a real fear become a paranoia?

When there is no longer any reason to fear.

After a while, it 's a relief to speak English to one another, or to English speaking tourists. One morning at breakfast we meet Doris Orgel, author of <u>The Devil in Vienna</u>, a fictionalized account of Doris' family's last days in Vienna before their escape when she was nine years old. She is in town to attend her sister Lotte's art opening at a gallery near the Hofburg, winter residence of the Hapsburgs, now housing government offices. The Austrian government, twisting inside out to make amends, as they do these days, invited her; a refugee's triumphant return.

Doris asks, "How are you feeling, Gerda?" The question is rhetorical. Doris knows that my mother cannot be feeling entirely well because she is not feeling entirely well.

"I'd forgotten," my mother says. "Vienna is a beautiful city."

"I can't wait to leave. I'm so sucked in. I can't bear the way I feel," Doris says, dolefully.

My mother agrees. The ambivalence is painful. To speak German again with such fluency, such delight, is painful. To hear everyone speak in dialect is painful.

One night, Chloe and I seek out a movie house that shows English language films without subtitles. This is my idea; I need a break.

We are standing on line with contemporary Austrians. I can hardly believe they exist. I can hardly believe they eat popcorn. We sit through Mr. Jones, though we've seen it before, and then walk back to the hotel through the castle grounds. A deserted landscape lit by a full moon. A soldier smiles at us, greets us with a subtle nod of his head. We feel safe.

Down on the Kärntnerstrasse, below the Opera, there is another scene. Young punks with multi-colored hair, beggars, and street musicians, travelers from all over Europe, passing through, English their lingua franca. The Viennese do not claim these "degenerates" as their own. We've been warned, in fact, that the Kärntnerstrasse, Vienna's main shopping street, is dangerous late at night and we should keep away, or take a taxi, if necessary. But rather than frightening, Chloe and I find this street fascinating. We stop to buy a raspberry glacé and to decipher placards. It's the week of the European Union vote, a watershed moment in Austrian history. Will Austria—a small country, isolated, enclosed, far from the sea—open its borders, open its markets? Many people we have talked to say they would like the Austrian borders to remain sealed against the "criminal element," a euphemism for "foreigner," *Ausländer*. A shrill anti-European Union campaign is being waged by the rightist, Jörg Haider – 44 year old, handsome, a political termagant—who warns of a loss of identity, political neutrality, jobs and money.

Not long ago, the Jews were considered *Ausländer* here, too. The word is familiar, a code. We begin to ask everyone we meet: How will you vote on the European Union? And make judgments about their politics, also their level of racism, based on the reply. "This country was never de-Nazified," my mother warns. "I can't believe they'll go into the Union."

At the opera one night (La Bohème, standing room), we strike up conversation, in English, with two travelers from Poland, both in medical school, and a young Viennese woman studying to become a primary school teacher. We discuss music, education, the weather, international youth culture, the European Union vote. And we are startled that this young demure Viennese woman will vote "No."

"Eighty percent of our trade is with Germany," she explains. "Why do we need anyone else? And then there's the criminal element, of course. Have you seen the Kärtnerstrasse at night? This is what the whole of Austria will look like if we go into the Union."

She is a pan-German, revised, celebrating the insularity and ethnocentrism of Germanic culture and values. Is this any different than the English or the French who, even as long-standing members of the European Union, are still struggling with issues of sovereignty? I'm not sure. Recent letter bomb campaigns have heightened the anxiety of the progressives in Austria. Vienna's Mayor, Helmut Zilk, lost part of his hand in a bomb blast in 1993. This is, to say the least, more serious than the genteel debates in British Parliament or the street demonstrations in Paris.

In the days of Empire, when Jews—the unassimilable "foreigners"—were protected by the Kaiser's edicts and patents and then later, after the First World War, under the Social Democrats, Vienna was a cosmopolitan, open, innovative city; now, my mother says, she observes that it is once again a provincial city, exuding *Schmäh*.

Paul Hofman, former reporter for The New York Times, and author of <u>The Viennese; Splendor, Twilight, Exile</u>, describes *Schmäh* as the use of language to deceive with a "knowing wink," a Viennese art. "What is Schmäh and what is truth?" he asks, reminding us of Kurt Waldheim's campaign autobiography which asserted that he was studying law in Vienna during the last years of the Second World War, "whereas he actually served as a Nazi intelligence officer in Yugoslavia and Greece."

Not far from our hotel are the spires of St. Stephen's Cathedral, the centripetal spoke of the city. Every morning, every evening we hear the tolling of bells. Austria, we are told, is still a profoundly conservative, Catholic country, resisting change. *Wien bleibt Wien*, a famous saying goes, without apology. Vienna stays

Vienna. Austria stays Austria.

If it's true, it's no different than it has been for centuries. Christian antisemitism flourished here. As soon as Hitler marched in, Archbishop Innitzer raised the Nazi flag from the cathedral's spires welcoming the Führer to Vienna.

Then, one morning, the vote is in. European Union, "Ja," a hopeful sign. For my mother, the city suddenly has a different aspect, less malignant and resonant with possibility.

"Austrians have shown once again they're much better than they believe they are," Social Democratic Chancellor Franz Vranitzky tells a crowd of reporters on the morning after the vote. Later in the day, vandals deface Jörg Haider posters with swastikas and scrawl Hitler-like mustaches on his face.

"Maybe it is difficult for us to accept the Austrians as flexible enough to change," I suggest that night at dinner. "Are the young people here able to relinquish their past? Are they cognizant enough of their past to relinquish it? Is this vote a fluke, or something more?"

What my mother says is true: the Austrian government was never forced by the occupying Allied powers to de-Nazify after the war. The government argued that all Austrians were victims of Hitler, not just the Jews. The Allies, eager to create a solid buffer zone against the Communist East, remained silent as the Austrians asserted their innocence.

## CHAPTER 6: JOSEFINENGASSE #4

We retrace steps. A school, a park, a cobbled street and arrive, finally, at Josefinengasse #4 in Vienna's Second District, the apartment house where my mother grew up and where my grandmother, Nanette, known to all who loved her as "Nina," spent the last days of her life.

Nanette buried my grandfather, Berthold, on April 15, 1942. Dazed when she left the cemetery after many sleepless nights at Berthold's hospital bedside, Nanette went to see her sister, Helene. "I have received my evacuation orders," Helene told her. This was the Nazi euphemism for deportation. And beyond deportation, the death camp.

Nanette decided to keep Helene company. Why did she do this? What were her thoughts? Perhaps she was too hungry and bereft to think clearly.

And, so, she volunteered for her own deportation.

We know this from one of Nanette's other sisters, Ida Sobotka, who survived Theresienstadt and lived to tell some of Nanette's story.

What if?

What if Nanette had stayed behind? What if she had managed to escape?

I would have a grandmother.

What if she had stayed behind and hidden somewhere in Vienna? Would someone, a neighbor perhaps, have denounced her and turned her in? Probably. William Shirer in his book <u>The Rise and Fall of the Third Reich</u>, has described the Viennese response after the German annexation as an "orgy of sadism," worse than anything he witnessed in Germany.

The S.S. was methodical and deadly, many were Austrian, the most infamous, after Hitler, was Adolf Eichmann. There were others: Kaltenbrunner, Globocnik, Seyss-Inquart. Three quarters of all death camp staff were Austrian. Many of the top camp commandants in Poland were Austrian. And the Austrian populace, the ordinary men and women, welcomed the annexation. One tenth of the Austrian population were active members of the Nazi party, more than in Germany.

Just before Berthold had his second heart attack, the S.S. came to the door. Once inside they took an inventory of all the valuables and noted who was living there. They were using the lists they stole from the Kultusgemeinde where most Jewish births, deaths and marriages were registered. They still are today. Protestants and Catholics, then and now, register elsewhere. Religious education, then and now, is obligatory in Austria. A confessed atheist must register as such to avoid mandated state religious education.

In Austria, decades before the Nazis came to power, a religious apartheid prevailed. Who was Jewish and who was not. Who was Christian and who was not. Who was converted and who was not. Meticulous records were kept awaiting Hitler. Then, in 1935, the Nuremberg racial laws were passed. They defined who was Jewish and who was "Aryan" by tracing ancestry. A person with one Jewish grandparent was considered Jewish. Despite assimilation and denial, Fritzi Burger was as endangered as the relatives she now refuses to acknowledge.

My grandfather, Berthold, was born in Holleshau, Czechoslovakia; he would not have been registered at the Kultusgemeinde.

But Nanette was. Certainly, their marriage was. I have seen the entry myself in the leather-bound ledger: February 12, 1905.

Still, it's tempting to construct a hypothetical scenario. What if? What if someone at Josefinengasse #4 had agreed to hide Nanette or helped her to escape during that small window of time after Berthold's death? In other countries—Holland, Belgium, France, Norway, Bulgaria, Denmark—there was resistance and heroic efforts to save the Jews, but there was none of any consequence in Austria. "We are sorry but there was no organized effort to save the Austrian Jews," writes Dr. Elisabeth Klamper, Director of the Archives of the Austrian Resistance, in a letter to me on October 25, 1994. I had to read the letter twice to make sure I understood.

I try to imagine how Nanette felt on the day she buried Berthold. Her daughter had already escaped to America, all communication with her silenced since the bombing of Pearl Harbor on December 7, 1941. No letters. No phone calls. The apartment was empty, the stillness disturbing. Berthold's socks at the foot of the bed, his encrusted toothbrush on the bathroom sink. No food in the larder after months of near starvation. Nanette packed a small valise, shut down all the windows, and walked out the door for the last time.

"It doesn't seem possible that the house is still standing," my mother says, "that life could go on as though nothing ever happened here. The visas we got from Ecuador never arrived. They were returned with a stamp—undeliverable—and a swastika. Nanette was already gone."

"This house is made of stone," I say. "Stones last, unless they are bombed. Did it always have a green door?"

"Who remembers doors?" my mother says.

The last time my mother was here was in 1973. During that visit she had not wanted to go inside. I was with her, too, as well as my stepfather and my husband, Jim, who had encouraged me to go when I had not wanted to. "This trip will be difficult for your mother," he had said. And, of course, he was right. But I was oddly indifferent at the time, and not paying attention to much of anything until we arrived at Josefinengasse #4. It was there that I first felt my mother's pain, then proceeded to bury it for another two decades.

On that first visit, the four of us stood across the street for a long time. What did my mother want to do? What scenario was she constructing about Nanette's last days? We waited patiently. A garbage truck passed, stopped, the men got out, emptied cans, talked cheerily to one another. When they were gone, we heard the sound of sweeping, a twigged broom brushing rhythmically against the stone pavement. The green door swung open revealing a courtyard and a very large woman wearing a kerchief. She looked up, saw us watching her, and continued with her work.

"It's Mrs. Schultz, the superintendent," my mother said, and before we could stop her, she was across the street and grabbing the broom out of the woman's hand. For a moment, we thought she was going to hit her with it. They talked heatedly, then fell laughing and weeping into each others' arms.

"We played hopscotch together," my mother said. "This isn't Mrs. Schultz, it's her daughter. We grew up together in this house."

"What does she know about Nanette?" I asked. "Did her family help her in any way?"

"They were Nazis," my mother said in English. "What would they have done to help Nanette?"

"Ask her," I insisted.

But my mother refused to ask.

\*\*\*\*\*

Now we are here again, in a reprise of our first visit. But we are also seeing Josefinengasse with different eyes. My mother is older, widowed for several months, and she is with her oldest grandchild, my daughter Chloe, with whom she has a special relationship. She is thinking lovingly of her other grandchildren, too, wishing they were here with us, and of her own childhood. This street, once resounding with the voices of innocent children, feels like a grave. Many whom my mother remembers as friend and playmate are now suspect.

"The Nazis wore white stockings. We thought we knew who they were," my mother says. "But on March 12, 1938, the day of the annexation, others came out of their hidey holes. The streets were lined with people waving Nazi flags and there were posters welcoming the Führer. At six in the morning, as I was leaving the hospital where I was interning, I saw a professor of mine, Dr. Hans Eppinger, putting up a poster, a bucket in one hand, a brush in the other. He was one of the Nazi doctors tried at Nuremberg."

Two days after Hitler marched in, Nanette was grabbed off the street by the S.S. on her way back from shopping and forced onto her hands and knees to scrub stones. "A young woman helped me," she told my mother when she finally returned home.

"Nanette was badly frightened.," my mother says. "That night at dinner we discussed what happened. Nanette knew it was serious, worse than any antisemitism we had experienced before. But Berthold had spent the afternoon in the cafe talking about the annexation with his brother, Arnold, and their political friends. 'This won't last,' he said. 'The Americans and the British will invade tomorrow.'"

After days of discussion, Nanette's intuition prevailed. She had felt the whip on her back, seen the anger in the S.S. soldier's eyes. It was decided that the young people should leave as quickly as possible. In an act beyond courage, my mother took a plane to Berlin where she obtained five false visas from a sympathetic French consul; one for her, one for my father, three others for his sister and brothers.

"They'll leave the old people alone," Berthold said refusing to be pessimistic or, some would now argue, realistic. "But the young people will be forced into labor for the Reich."

Berthold was nearly right about forced labor. The Nazi plan had always been to work the Jews to death. Those that survived forced labor would be exterminated.

\*\*\*\*\*

This is a poor neighborhood now, housing guest workers from the East who have had their own share of trouble here, not as bad as in Germany, but trouble nonetheless. We push open the green door and enter the courtyard, musty with the smell of cooking.

"This is where we used to bang our carpets," my mother says.

"No vacuum cleaners when I was a child."

Up a flight of stairs, there is a door with a brass name plate: Yusuf Albayark.

"Do you want to go in?" I ask.

"I want to go in," Chloe says, not waiting for my mother's reply.

"I'll knock," my mother says, holding Chloe's hand tightly.

We are lucky, there is someone at home. Without even a "Who is it?" the door is opened. It is Yusuf Albayark himself, a man perhaps in his forties, thin, frail, with an enormous indentation on the left side of his skull, the result, apparently, of a horrific accident at work. We find this out later, of course, but as we enter the apartment, which he has offered us as though it is ours, he smiles, and introduces us to his wife. Would we like some coffee? Something to eat? Would we like to see the apartment?

We are communicating in German, but there are lapses in historical sequence. It's not clear if Yusuf has ever heard the word "Holocaust."

"I'm so glad you're here," my mother says, as Yusuf graciously offers us some candy and begins to show us around the newly renovated apartment. "If there had been a Viennese family here, I would have been upset."

The Albayarks are Turkish Christians, refugees from poverty, living in a Third World Diaspora. The irony does not escape us.

We admire the wallpaper, the new stall shower, the bunk beds, a picture of Yusuf's son and his new bride. My mother shows us where she slept, where she played. Yusuf's wife trills when my mother says, "death camps," relives with her the story of Nanette's last days. It is the beginning of a new openness, voicing the horrors, an expiation. And there are parallels here, the comfort of knowing that so much of human experience—bitterness, pain, joy—is universal.

"My father is here," Yusuf says. "Would you like to say hello?"

He leads us to the living room, where his elderly father is resting on a settee.

"You're fortunate," my mother says.

On the trolley back into town, its route unchanged, we pass the Taborkine movie house where my mother saw Al Jolson on the giant screen in 1927 before her life was ruptured by the war. She loved the movies, went there often. This was her neighborhood, her childhood turf. The smell of the streets is as familiar to her as her own breath.

## CHAPTER 7: STONES

Auschwitz is my grandmother Nanette's grave. She was murdered, her name lost to history in a mass grave. We do not know the exact day she died or how long she lived inside the camp after she arrived. There are no remains, no body, no clothing, no prayer books, no tombstones. Only ashes.

Berthold, however, is buried in Vienna. We can find his grave because we know when he died and when Nanette buried him. Soon after, she went on vacation with her sister, Helene—to Auschwitz. As the Zentralfriedhof is an orthodox cemetery, a headstone could not be put up right away. Usually, a ceremony is performed some months later (within a year) to "unveil" a stone. The unveiling marks the end of the mourning period. But, for my family, Berthold's death was the beginning of a mourning period without end, a kind of purgatory. My mother in America, Nanette in Auschwitz, Ida and Arnold in Theresienstadt. Our lists go on and on.

When I ask my mother why she did not visit Berthold's grave in 1973, she says, without sentiment, "The dead are dead." Her views on the subject have not essentially changed but because Chloe is in Vienna and has used the word "closure," with reference to a visit to the cemetery, my mother seems more flexible. At least she is listening. Closure. How does this sound, I ask her?

"How can there be closure," she asks. "Do you think a visit to the cemetery will give me closure?"

And there is more: snide comments about my sentimentality and Chloe's quiet persistence.

Now she is angry because we are forcing her. She wishes she were back in Connecticut. She wishes she had never come.

"We are going to the cemetery," I say. "Stay behind in the hotel or join us, as you wish."

I am finding her insufferable and have lost my patience.

Back to the Kultusgemeinde to peruse the records. Berthold is buried in Vienna's Eleventh District, at the Zentralfriedhof cemetery, Section 20, Row 23, Grave 21. We are warned by the clerk that the grave may be unmarked, that the cemetery is untended, and that the caretaker, Josef Kohut, is overwhelmed with correspondence from refugees. The old Jewish section of the Zentralfriedhof (Central Cemetery) has been badly neglected primarily because there are no survivors in Vienna to look after the graves. Recently, a group of young men and women began a clean-up project but it is limited and sporadic. Josef must also organize new burials as there is, lest we have forgotten, a living Jewish community in Vienna.

*****

A ride of nearly an hour to the outskirts of the city. One cemetery following another. Men and women in black suits carrying flowers. Is there ever a day when there is not a funeral? We debark the trolley at Zentralfriedhof at mid-day. The sun is high. There is no wind. My mother has decided to come.

Josef Kohut, a small round man in his mid-forties, welcomes us into his office.

"Apologies for not being computerized," he says impishly, half in German, half Yiddish. He is referring to a small notebook where he has found Berthold's name. It is splattered with food stains and blue ink.

"I hope you've made a photocopy of that," I say, feeling somewhat impish myself. Josef's irreverence is welcome and puts me in a better mood..

Josef's round cheeks expand into a smile. He's alone in this office most of the day and appreciates visitors, though they seem to arrive all in a bunch. His English is good.

"Are you a rabbi?," my mother asks. She has little or no patience with orthodox Jews. And she resents the fact that her father had to be buried in this orthodox cemetery, that there was no choice. He wasn't a religious man.

Josef laughs. "I'm an orthodox Jew, but not a rabbi. Come, I will show you on this map where to find your father's grave and point you in the right direction. Then I will leave you. If you need me, return to the office."

"Will the grave be unmarked?" I ask.

"Probably unmarked," he says.

We leave Josef behind to begin our search. There are a few headstones, eroded, nearly impossible to read. The rest is a desert of desiccated, mole-tunneled earth. Row upon row of straw covered mounds, littered with garbage, as soft underfoot as a swamp.

Are we in the right section? Is this Row 23? Chloe volunteers to count graves.

"Where is Chloe? I want to leave," my mother says, distressed, as I am, that she has disappeared from view. Suddenly, the world is still, time frozen. I feel a rush of agonizing fear and loss and all I want to do is cry. Worse, I have lost sight of my own child and the panic has made me inconsolable. Isn't this what Nanette must have felt like that day in 1938 when my mother left for Paris, never to return?

Nearly hysterical, I call Chloe's name. And then, finally, she reappears.

"I'm lost," she says. But what she means, simply, is that she cannot unravel the labyrinth of unmarked graves. She has not, as yet, felt the vertigo of disappearance without return, primarily because I have been protecting her from it all her life. And so she is able to remain level-headed. For the first time, I feel that Chloe, one generation removed from the Holocaust, is looking after us and that her serenity is life-sustaining.

"We have to go back and speak to the caretaker," she says.

"Mr. Kohut we can't find Berthold's grave," I say when we return to the office. I'm edgy and can't conceal it, though I have infinite patience compared to my mother. She wants to leave immediately, she says. It's not worth it.

Once again, that phrase.

"Whether or not we find Berthold's grave is of no consequence," she continues. "What's dead is dead, what's gone is gone."

"Sit down. I will be with you in a moment," Josef says. He has taken note of our distress, but he is on the telephone arranging a funeral.

"My mother wants to leave," I say, interrupting him. It already feels as though we have been here too long. "But my daughter and I don't want to leave until we have found Berthold's grave."

There is another visitor here, Harry Franklin, also from New York City.

"I can't find my father's grave," he says.

"So this is not unusual," my mother says, consoled by Harry's warm, calm presence and the knowledge that her experience is shared. All those other abandoned bodies whose relatives were deported before headstones could be raised.

While we wait, Chloe helps Harry fix his camera.

"Sit, sit. Give me a minute, I will take you to find the graves," Josef Kohut says, kindly. It is obvious he has done this many times before.

Harry Franklin is wearing a black crepe paper yarmulke which has wilted on his head in the hot sun. His smooth skinned face is streaked with sweat. And he's carrying a duffel with a collection of theater programs from before the war, all signed by famous Austrian actors. He was only 17 when he fled and had the presence of mind to take the collection with him. After the cemetery, he's meeting with a buyer, who is interested. But first he must find his father's grave. Like my mother, nearly everyone else in his family was murdered in the camps.

Josef Kohut is our point man. I am beside him, my mother, Chloe and Harry Franklin, a few steps behind. We are walking underneath giant oak trees where a flock of crows, as full-bodied as vultures, nest in thick, lush branches.

"My first wife is buried here." Josef says, turning to me, his impish smile metamorphosed into deep sadness. "Over there. In the new section. She was killed in the PLO attack on the Stadttempel in Vienna's First District in 1981, on a Saturday, after services. A grenade. Machine gun fire. I was standing on the steps right next to her. She died instantly. She was one of two who died that day.

There were many injured.

"It was a terrorist attack. It could have happened anywhere," I say, sensing that the revelation is a desire for comfort. "They attacked the World Trade Center in New York."

"I know that," Josef says. He seems more resigned, than angry. "It was so absurd. She converted to Judaism to marry me."

We are now in the post-war section of the cemetery. Ida Sobotka is buried here. Her grave is clearly marked. And there are other, more elaborate graves with fresh flowers, unheard of in an orthodox cemetery, but Josef permits it. He's an easygoing man.

"Did you know that orthodox Jews can't be buried next to secular Jews?" he asks. "They would not rest in peace. They would turn in their graves."

"My grandfather was a freethinker," I say.

"I was free once, too," Josef says, "I was born here in Vienna. My family survived the war in Shanghai. Then I lived in Israel. In Israel and America a Jew can be free. I don't know why I came back here. I can look at you and see you are free. You eat what you want. You marry whom you please. I am married now again with four children."

*****

I have a picture of my mother standing on Berthold's grave, or the mound of earth Josef Kohut has assured us is his grave. She looks forlorn, which is the way she feels, the way we all feel. Perhaps she is standing on Berthold's stomach or eyes or chin.

"I have found his grave, now what?" she says, and we have an argument about whether or not we should spend the money for a headstone.

"The mourning period cannot end until a stone is unveiled," I remind her. I believe rituals are important, even if we create our own. "We are here to put Berthold and Nanette to rest."

"I would rather spend the money on my grandchildren," she says, bitterly. Harry Franklin agrees. He is not going to put a headstone up either, though he will discuss it with his sister when he returns to America.

But I do not feel at peace with this, nor does Chloe, who leaves us in search of stones and pebbles to place, as a gesture of remembrance, on Berthold's grave.

*****

Back in the center of town, we stop by the *Mahnmal gegen Krieg und Faschismus*, the Monument Against War and Fascism, unveiled by the Austrian government, on November 24, 1988. In German, the word Mahnmal means warning or reminder, rather than the over-simplified translation, monument. The central image is of an old Jew crouching down on his hands and knees scrubbing stones. A sign, hidden behind some bushes too far away from the monument for most people to notice reads, in part, "The first to fall victim to the Nazi regime were political opponents and Jews. After 12 March 1938, many Jews were forced out of their homes and into the streets to clean away political slogans. The figure of the kneeling Jew is to remind us of these acts of humiliation."

The front of the square is bordered by the "Gate of Violence," carved from the granite thousands of prisoners carried over the "stairs of death," at the Mauthausen death camp. And there are other stones here, too, smaller stones visitors have placed on the old Jew's back. And a bouquet of flowers shrunk to straw in the summer heat.

Yet many visitors pass and do not know what they are seeing here, or what the four-part sculpture represents. Unfortunately, though extraordinarily beautiful and very moving, the sculpture is too abstract to be meaningful to those who know nothing about the Holocaust. And the signage is inadequate. The one directly in front of the monument is in German without translation and says only, "On this site was the Phillipphof [apartment building] which was bombed [by the Allies] on March 12, 1945. The people that were hidden in the cellar were killed. This monument is dedicated to all the victims of war and Fascism."

There are travelers here from many parts of the world, but no Austrians. The local Viennese stay away; this is a tourist attraction and they don't take it seriously we've been told. Sometimes, usually late at night, young people, punks and tearaways, can be seen sitting on the old Jew's back.

"They feel ashamed" my mother says, her eyes swelled with tears. "That's why they don't come."

"Why sit on the Jews' back," I ask.

"Perhaps they can't decipher the Monument," Chloe suggests. "They don't know it's a Jew. Or maybe they don't know anything about the Nazi era. Or they don't care. Or it's too long ago. Or they're ashamed, as Baba says, and they don't want to be reminded. They need a guide, a guru. And there aren't any."

Though she could not cry at the cemetery, my mother is able to cry here in the presence of these powerful archetypal forms, and willing to show others that she can cry.

"I'm glad this Monument is here," she says.

Chloe befriends a group of young American tourists traveling with ES tours. Their Austrian guide has no idea what this Monument is. And so Chloe explains, and introduces them to her grandmother.

Later, though we have taken many photographs, we go into the local shops to search for a postcard of the Monument, but there is none to be found. A copyright problem? No one seems to know.

But a discussion with Dr.Bernhard Denscher, Head of the Department of Cultural Affairs in Vienna is illuminating. "In my opinion this work of art should be more than just a tourist sight," he told me. "It should provide food for thought and incite the beholder to pause and linger. If this is the case, he will certainly also be interested in the discreetly placed information sign."

And, of course, there are no postcards. This is not a monument, not a tourist sight; it is a warning.

The Viennese are schmoozers and have an answer for everything. It was the most articulate rationalization I'd heard in days.

## CHAPTER 8: GLOVES

Every day on her way home from high school, my mother passed the Haslinger glove factory in Vienna's Second District. This factory was an integral part of the landscape of my mother's youth. Bertha Haslinger, wife of the owner, was one of my grandmother's older sisters, much older in fact. Nanette was still quite young when Bertha married Joseph Haslinger, a wealthy man who owned the glove factory and, at one time, at least twenty-five retail outlet stores throughout Austria. By the time Bertha married Joseph, there were only two retail stores left, one attached to the factory itself, the other on the Rotenturmstrasse in the shadow of St. Stephen's Cathedral.

Over the years, Joseph Haslinger became the unofficial family patriarch; benevolent, caring, and reliable. When someone in the family was out of work, he gave them a job. My grandfather, Berthold, worked for him after his own frankfurter factory failed. He became a salesman, traveling primarily in Yugoslavia. And my grandmother, Nanette, worked in the Rotenturmstrasse store with Bertha and Joseph's daughter, Hedy.

As often happens in large, rambling families, Nanette was closer in age to her niece than to her own sister. Not only did Nanette and Hedy work together, they were also friends. My mother remembers Hedy well. Hedy was also a part-time actress, larger than life and comical. She married another actor who was Catholic and converted to Catholicism. Hedy's daughter, Dorrith, is our only living relative in Austria. We have plans to see her and many questions to ask. But first we must visit the glove store.

I've done some research and discovered that the Mr. Johann Slunsky, who took over the store after the annexation, had been an apprentice in the Haslinger factory. Questions therefore remain: Was Mr. Slunsky the Nazi appointed *Commissar Leiter*, the "commissar manager?" This was a Nazi euphemism for the members of the Austrian Nazi Party who confiscated Jewish property after the annexation. They were usually people who worked in the establishment and were familiar with it. Hard to imagine an apprentice taking over the factory. And that the descendants of this person still own the glove store in the center of Vienna. Greed, lust, fulfillment of envy. It is unconscionable.

My mother is eager for this particular confrontation.

We set out early one morning when we are feeling refreshed from another night at the opera. People are rushing to work and cafes are opening their doors. On the left side of the Rotenturmstrasse, a sign is clearly visible at #23 – *Handschuhe* (gloves). "It used to be *Haslinger Handschuhe*," my mother says.

The store is narrow and very warm. The three of us can just barely squeeze in. There's an L-shaped glass counter, floor to ceiling boxes filled with gloves, a wooden chair, the pungent smell of leather. A woman is behind the counter showing gloves to a customer. She is a tall, robust, middle-aged woman with a ruddy complexion, dark brown hair and a friendly smile.

I pull out my notebook, feel the heat emanating from my mother's skin. She introduces herself immediately as a relation of the Haslingers.

The woman looks alarmed. She calls her mother, Frau Johann Slunsky, wife of the apprentice, out of the back room.

Hands offered in greeting, a chair pulled forward, glasses of water offered, none of which cools our efflorescing rage.

"*Gnädige, Frau*, I remember you," the younger woman, Johanna Slunsky, says. "You were here with your husband some years ago, no?"

This is true. My mother came here with my stepfather in the early 1980's, looked around, asked a few questions. This is the visit Johanna Slunsky remembers. No mention was made of the Holocaust, of how Nanette or the Haslingers died, only that Nanette had worked in the store and was related to the original owners.

"This is my daughter. She's a journalist and works for the American government," my mother says. "And my granddaughter, but she can't understand German."

"I'm a journalist but I don't work for the government," I explain, my hand on my mother's in an effort to calm her down. I cannot allow her to misrepresent me, though I fully understand the temptation.

Johanna, the daughter, is very upset. We are upsetting her mother. Why are we here? What is it we want? Perhaps we are planning to make a restitution claim?

This is impossible, I say. The statute of limitations ran out in 1985.

So what exactly is our purpose here?

"What happened to this store after the annexation," my mother asks.

"*Gnädige Frau*. We do not know," Johanna Slunsky says.

I am less than a foot from Mrs. Slunsky's face, so close we can smell each others' sweat.

"Let me tell you what happened to the Haslingers," my mother says.

"*Gnädige Frau.*"

"The Haslingers died in the Warsaw Ghetto. They went there with another daughter, Stella, and her family in search of safety after the "Aryanization." Hedy and Nanette, who worked in this store, stayed behind. Nanette, my mother, was murdered in Auschwitz. Hedy and her daughter, Dorrith, survived the war in Vienna. Dorrith is still alive."

"A shame," Johanna Slunsky says. "Would you like some more water *Gnädige Frau?*"

"*Frau Doktor,*" my mother says. "I'm a graduate of the University of Vienna."

"*Frau Doktor,*" Johanna says, her head bent in mock servility.

Titles are still important in Vienna, signaling class and status. *Gnädige Frau* means simply "My Dear Woman." It is a polite but obsequious form of address. Or it can be condescending or bitter.

*Frau Doktor*, my mother insists. She is turning whatever repertoire of knives she holds which is, in fact, our purpose here.

"Ask them how they got the store," I say.

"We bought it," Johanna says. "Naturally. It is not as large as it was originally. The building was damaged in the Allied bombing. We changed the configuration..."

But we are not interested in renovation.

"Where is Mr. Slunsky?," my mother asks. "Didn't he work for Mr. Haslinger?"

"He began as an apprentice at the factory," Johanna says. "The factory was bombed in 1945."

"And where is he now?," I ask.

"Dead," Johanna Slunsky says, definitively, perhaps hoping this will put an end to our questions and that we will go away, never to return.

"My husband is dead, too," my mother says. She says this as though she is ripping candy out of a child's hand. The German word for dead—*tot*—more emotionally charged than its English equivalent.

Denials, fawning smiles. Was Mr. Slunsky the Commissar Leiter?

No, he was not, Mrs. Slunsky says.

This is a *Schmäh*, a dissembling. Slunsky was not a Commissar, but he was complicit in the theft of the store. I have documents from the Austrian State Archive in my bag; Ernest Seemann and Otto Zenker, long standing employees of the Haslinger Glove Factory, were the appointed *Commissare* of the factory. Zenker "bought" the store. And Slunsky, the apprentice, "bought" the store from Zenker probably because Zenker did not want it; he was too busy with the factory. Without the label Commissar, so easily relinquished, the Slunsky's have convinced themselves they bought the store — legally.

"I think we should go," Chloe says. She's been standing patiently on the sidelines, unable to understand most of what is being said. But she has observed the semiotics of the situation, felt the heat, interpreted gestures.

What else can we hope to accomplish here? What is it we want? Revenge? Confession?

Or perhaps an apology.

More offers of Viennese tap water—cold, clear—the best in

the world, according to the Viennese.

My mother is not ready to leave. There is another game she wants to play. What she wants is a pair of driving gloves. Would they have her size?

"*Gnädige Frau. Frau Doktor. Natürlich.* Naturally."

Now there is a large plastic box on the table and the odor of leather mingled with our sweat. My mother is trying on gloves—elegant, beautifully crafted — and she is remembering her father's bulging carry case before he set out on his sales trips. When he returned, the gloves were replaced with books for my mother's library, a magical transformation.

"Did I tell you my mother, who worked in this store, was murdered in Auschwitz?" my mother says, turning the gloves over in her hands, examining them, sniffing them. "And that the Haslingers, my aunt and uncle who owned this store and the factory, were murdered in the Warsaw Ghetto?"

"Shame," Johanna whispers. "*Frau Doktor,* may I show you some more gloves?"

"I like these. How much?"

"Five hundred schillings." Nearly fifty American dollars.

"Too much. Would you lower your price?"

This is a hypothetical question. My mother has no intention of buying anything. She is winking at me, telling me this in English under her breath. They should give her a pair because they owe her something, an atonement. Why don't they understand?

"*Gnädige Frau*, three hundred schillings is as low as I can go," Johanna Slunsky says. Her mother has been observing this exchange silently. More than likely she and Johanna understand English quite well and have therefore grasped what my mother has said.

A firm click. Johanna shuts the box and puts it away. No more bargaining. No more Jews.

"You will be hearing from us," my mother says, ominously.

"*Gnädige Frau.*"

I put my notebook away.

"Ask them if they'd let us take their photograph," I say. "I'd like a picture of them in front of the store. Under the sign."

"My daughter would like a photograph," my mother says with her own perfected *Schmäh* smile.

"*Gnädige Frau.*"

Afterwards, I shake Johanna's and Mrs. Slunsky's hand and thank them, politely, for their time. I tell them I will send them a copy of the photograph, but I have not, as yet, done so.

## Chapter 9: Dorrith

On the second morning of our stay in Vienna, Dorrith Wagner, our only living relative in Austria, arrives at the hotel. Dorrith is sixty-eight years old, strong and tall, with the high cheekbones and broad lips of my grandmother Nanette's side of the family. Her mother, Hedy, and my grandmother, Nanette, worked in the glove store together.

Like Fritzi Burger, Dorrith grew up a Catholic. Her mother, Hedy, converted to Catholicism when she married Dorrith's father and Dorrith was baptized when she was a baby. Unlike Fritzi, Dorrith survived the war in Vienna, still lives here, and reconnected with whatever family was left after the war. She has kept up a correspondence with our cousin, Franzi, in Israel and with my mother in America. She was on holiday when I was last in Vienna in 1973, so I never met her.

Let me put our relationship in context: Dorrith's grandmother and my grandmother were sisters. This makes Dorrith my second cousin, as far removed from me in the family tree as Fritzi is to my mother; their grandmothers were also sisters. My mother and Dorrith are first cousins once removed.

My mother has always spoken lovingly of Dorrith. She babysat for her and often went on summer vacations with Dorrith, her parents and the Haslinger grandparents. As my mother got older, she was hired, more formally, as a paid *au pair* for Dorrith or any other young children who were around, another example of Haslinger generosity. But these financial arrangements didn't change my mother's devotion to the younger children in her family, especially Dorrith, whom she absolutely adored.

Now, sitting on high backed chairs in the lounge of the Hotel Kaiserin Elisabeth, a portrait of the Victorian Empress herself staring down on us benevolently, my mother has gone to the bathroom, Chloe is snapping pictures, and Dorrith is whispering to me in German. Is my mother very sad living alone in the house now that her husband has died? Can she walk well enough to do some sightseeing today?

"My mother's cane is a placebo," I assure her. "She's stronger than all of us."

Dorrith can understand English though speaking is more difficult for her. I have the exact opposite problem—I can understand German but not speak—thus enabling us to communicate directly, without the mediation of a translator, in two languages.

When my mother returns, she tells Dorrith about our visit to the glove store. Dorrith seems incredulous.

"You visited the store?"

"Why, yes if course. Chloe and Carol wanted to see it."

"It must have been upsetting."

"My blood was boiling," my mother says.

"Gerda, why are you doing this? Why are you stirring yourself up this way? This can't be good for your health."

"It's very good for my health. Why are you whispering, Dorrith?"

Dorrith stops talking. She looks disgruntled.

"Why is Carol taking notes?," she asks.

"Carol's writing a book."

I put my notebook away. I look around. We are alone in the lounge.

"I'm sorry if I've made you uncomfortable," I say. "But we need to have these conversations. There are so many unanswered questions. I am curious. Did you make a restitution claim after the war?"

"The factory was bombed. The glove store wasn't worth anything. We were alone. Everyone tot. There were still Nazis everywhere."

"I see."

"Let's go to the Hofburg. The crown jewels will take your mind off the past," Dorrith says.

I expect my mother to say, "You're right, it's not worth it, I'm glad you didn't make a restitution claim," but she remains silent. Since the visit to the cemetery, I have felt a shift in her refugee persona. No longer victim, she is calling everything and everyone to account, even Dorrith. She does not want her to whisper. She does not want her to be afraid.

On the way to the Hofburg, we pass the Monument Against War and Fascism. My mother wants to stop again, but Dorrith pulls her away.

*****

Crown jewels. For a while, Dorrith and my mother are young again, holding hands, star struck at the magnificence of sapphires, rubies and pearls. There is an illusion here of security and continuity and it is comforting. Life was predictable under the monarchy, even for Jews.

At the end of the tour, the Hofburg visitors spill out through the gate onto the Michaelerplatz where there is an archaeological dig taking place. Layers of history are being stripped away, past antiquity and the Roman occupation, deeper and deeper into the rock. Questions are being asked, answers sought.

"We're also on an archaeological dig," I say to Dorrith over lunch at the famous Griensteidl Cafe where a literary coffeehouse group known as the "Young Vienna" once gathered. What questions would these intelligentsia be asking if they were still here today?

*****

We don't know exactly what we are going to see from the top of the mountain on this gray, overcast day, but we take the metro out to Heiligenstadt, a northern suburb, where Dorrith says she will meet us to take a bus into the Vienna Woods. The woods consist of two hills, the northernmost spur of the Alps. We are headed for the Kahlenberg (elevation 1,585 feet). Dorrith has urged us to come, eager to spend another full day with us before our departure for Prague. There is a subscript to our plans—the sadness of an impending good-bye and the realization that Dorrith, because of her obligations, will not be able to travel to America any time soon.

Dorrith points out the sights, the Danube, of course, which is never blue but a muddy gray, flowing like a great thick snake through the flat countryside. Another *Schmäh*, says Paul Hofmann. A "pleasant lie," that the Danube is not blue at all.

At the summit, we meander through a church, admire a Black Madonna, notice the chimney of a recycling plant in the distance playfully decorated in bright colors by Hundertwasser, the well known contemporary Austrian artist. It's an anomaly in the regulated, predictable landscape. Zoning regulations, strictly enforced for decades, has kept Vienna pollution free, with green farmland abutting the city on all sides. And there are few high-rises to trap the stale summer air.

Over lunch, I want to talk to Dorrith about the Haslinger glove store and what transpired there between us and the Slunsky women. But, for some reason, my mother is reluctant to begin. What is it she fears? What is it she cannot ask? But now I remember. The question flashed into my mind when we were in the store: *What did Dorrith's mother, Hedy, do to save Nanette? She was converted, married to a Catholic. What, if anything  could she have done without endangering her life and that of her daughter?*

Our time is limited, our departure imminent. When will we have the opportunity to talk with Dorrith, one of the last people to see Nanette alive, face to face again?

Reluctantly, my mother agrees to press Dorrith to answer questions.

Dorrith begins, again, in a whisper. "We went to the apartment on Josefinengasse one day and Nanette was gone," she says. "I have such fond memories. We visited Berthold and Nanette often, or they visited us. Then one day Berthold died and Nanette was gone, just gone. It was a bad time for all of us."

What do the Slunsky women know of such terror? They had the store. They were content.

Twelve years old at the time of the annexation, Dorrith spent her teen years, years when young girls are normally carefree, living in a reign of terror.

Under duress, when the factory was being "Aryanized," Joseph

Haslinger had filled out forms. On one such form, dated August 8, 1938, on the line marked "children," Joseph wrote that he had "three full Jewish daughters." "Two are married," the typewritten words say, "living away from home, and a third, divorced, lives with us. There is also a grandchild."

The divorced daughter was Hedy, the grandchild, Dorrith. The fact that they were both Catholic became meaningless with this declaration.

After the Haslingers fled to Warsaw, Hedy and Dorrith moved into their Catholic in-law's home where they hid out for the duration of the war.

Difficult as it is, we allow the urgency of our questioning to subside. There is no answer to our question: What could Hedy have done to help Nanette? It is moot.

The view of the valley from the top of the mountain is breathtaking. That we are here together is a small miracle.

Dorrith is amused by our vegetarian choices: a plate of boiled potatoes, a cucumber salad.

She pulls out an envelope of photographs: A picture of Nanette, a picture of Hedy, a picture of Nanette and Dorrith at the seaside, and hands them to my mother.

"I want you to have them," she says. "Take them to America."

This is a wonderful gift.

"And here are some envelopes for the children. Austrian schillings. To buy something they would very much like."

Two envelopes are presented. One for Chloe, another for my sister's children.

"After the war, everyone in the family dead, except for me and my mother, except for you and Renate and Franzi."

I had forgotten or perhaps never realized it before – Dorrith is a survivor, too.

And she lives in Vienna, my mother does not. The memory of the war is with her every day. And the fear has not dissipated. This is the meaning of Dorrith's whispers and her mother's reluctance to make a restitution claim. To do so would have announced to her neighbors that she was a Jew.

At the trolley stop in Grinsig, where the Austrian wine harvest is celebrated, it is time to say good-bye. My mother wants to buy Dorrith a plant for her apartment. We linger in front of the florist while she pays. And then we hug each other. I am weeping, of course, as I do at every parting, imagining as many children of survivors do, that all leave takings are final. Chloe is crying, too. Despite the language barrier, she has felt a very strong connection with Dorrith. "You and Chloe are a piece of my family," Dorrith wrote to me after we returned to America. "I feel as though I have known you all my life." Chloe and I both feel the same way.

*****

My mother's eyes are dry.

"Did you cry when you left Vienna," I ask, as we descend out of a pastoral landscape into the urban labyrinth. Chloe has her arm around me and my head is on her shoulder. We turn around and see Dorrith waving.

"I refused to cry," my mother says. "I thought maybe I wouldn't see my father again. He had a bad heart and probably would not have survived a long journey. But I assumed, beyond question, that I would see my mother again."

"How did they survive all those years?" Chloe asks. "Nanette and Berthold lived under the Nazi occupation for nearly four years. That's a long time."

"What did they <u>have</u> to do to survive," I ask as the trolley rambles down the Ring.

My mother is pointing out the sights, ignoring us. These are questions she prefers remain unanswered. Like Dorrith, she is adept at changing the subject. And she is impatient with my tears.

When my mother doesn't cry, I cry for her, as well as for myself, the emotion work of a survivor's daughter. Not out of pity or self pity, or fear or frustration, but out of attentiveness and a desire to know, beyond cerebral knowing.

## CHAPTER 10: CLEAN STREETS, DIRTY HISTORY

My mother studied medicine at the University of Vienna. There were other women studying medicine at the time, but not many.

Antisemitism was endemic at the university since the Jews were first permitted entrance in the 1880's. Jews were excluded from fraternities, libraries, and professional organizations. But exclusions didn't prevent them from getting ahead. In fact, they were irrepressible. By 1910, half of the medical student body and faculty were Jewish, the faculty mostly converted, assimilated Jews.

By 1930, one year before my mother began her studies, the more benign form of religious antisemitism had evolved into a more radical, racist form. The University of Vienna had a Pan-Germanic rector, Wenzel Gleispach, who tried to divide the university into four "nations"; "German," "non-German," "mixed," and "other." A student would be considered non-German unless he could prove that his or her parents and all four grandparents had been baptized. It was a blatant attempt to transform *de facto* religious discrimination at the university into a *de jure* racial/religious apartheid.

Gleispach's ideas were not new ones, nor were they invented by Hitler who was already in full voice in Germany by 1930; they had permeated European antisemitic discourse for centuries. By the time Hitler came to power, there were more than 430 antisemitic associations and 700 antisemitic periodicals in Austria and Germany, all espousing views similar to Gleispach's.

Although Gleispach's plan passed the academic senate at the

university by an easy margin, it was struck down on June 23, 1931 by the Austrian Supreme Court. That afternoon, the Nazi students rioted, viciously attacking with truncheons and fists whatever "Jewish" and "Socialist" students they could find. "Jews," "Socialists," "Bolsheviks," were often used as interchangeable epithets by the Nazis who believed in a world-wide Jewish "conspiracy."

Bodies spilled onto the steps leading onto the Ring, the magnificent regal avenue that belts the city, where police waited to arrest whoever fell into their arms. They had no jurisdiction inside the university.

My mother remembers that the university was shut down for the rest of the term. Only students taking exams were permitted into the building.

On other occasions, lectures were punctuated by shouted epithets, "JUDEN RAUS," (Jews out), often deteriorating into brawls. On calmer days, there was, simply, harassment.

Women were not spared the brutality or harassment of their Nazi peers, or their Nazi professors. The dean of the medical school, Dr. Hans Eppinger, who was later tried at Nuremberg, failed my mother on her internal medicine oral exams by asking her a trick question based on his own "research," which was not recorded in any of the assigned texts. Six months later, she took the exam again with another professor and passed.

My mother learned to keep a low profile and to slip away when she felt endangered, a foreshadowing of survival protocol. But from time to time she felt safe enough to resist or speak out. Once she set off a stink bomb in organic chemistry lab when she was placed at a table with white-stockinged Nazis. Once she threw harmless acid onto a student who called her a dirty Jew. She told him the acid would burn him irreparably and he believed her and ran terrified from the room.

After she graduated in 1937, my mother's uncle, Arnold, who was also a doctor, managed to get her an internship at the S. Canning Childs Spital (Hospital) near the university. This was no easy task; Jews were not normally permitted to work there. After annexation, she was asked, politely, to leave, but not until she trained her "Aryan" replacement. My mother did this for the benefit of the patients while, at the same time, applying for a job at the Rothschild Hospital, a Jewish hospital where only Jewish doctors worked. There she was advised to continue her training as a nurse, rather than as a doctor, as eventually all Jewish doctors would be dismissed from there, too.

My mother met my father at the Rothschild Hospital, where he was a highly regarded eye surgeon, and they fell in love. Their affair was passionate and bold, a fireball of desire and hope in what had become a desolate and forbidding landscape.

Traveling back and forth to the hospital was dangerous and my mother carried a letter with her from the Medical Association in case she was picked up:

*It is ordered by the above organization [of Viennese doctors] that the service of physicians has to continue undisturbed, even at night. Working physicians should not be hindered by orders to clean the streets.*

The seal of the new Nazi *Kommisariche Leitung* (commissar manager) of the organization is affixed, dated 1 April 1938.

Eventually, my mother quit her job at the hospital to make preparations for departure. She did this reluctantly, as did my father.

My father's family was wealthy. They owned a saw mill in a small town near the Hungarian border. This was immediately confiscated by the S.S., and they fled into the city, prevailing on family and friends to take them in. Berthold and Nanette offered to shelter them for a while, though their apartment was very small and, for a brief time, they all lived together at Josefinengasse #4 – all my grandparents, my mother and father, his sister and brothers — until everyone decided what they wanted to do, what they were able to do, financially and otherwise. It was decided all the young people would leave and Berthold, with his heart condition, should stay. Nanette, of course, would remain behind with him. Eventually, my father's parents left for Innsbruck where the trail of their search for safety is lost. All we know is that they, too, were murdered in Auschwitz.

*****

My mother wants to take the trolley around the Ring to the University. She's been visualizing this particular excursion for days, and looking forward to it. Despite the difficulties endured during her university years, she has fond memories she wants to share with us.

"How clean Vienna is," she says, thinking of New York, as the trolley rounds the bend onto the section of the Ring named after Dr. Karl Lueger, Vienna's turn-of-the century antisemitic mayor. Why would the Viennese choose to name a prominent thoroughfare after such a man?

"No *Schmutz*," I say, using the German word for dirt. I am saying this tongue-in-cheek as I always find Germanic cleanliness disturbing. Over the years it has become a metaphor in my mind for the tyranny of Fascist obedience and the Austro-German propensity to sanitize history, sweep truths away, and exonerate guilt and shame.

In Vienna, everything is very clean and tidy, to the naked eye. At the Cafe Sacher, we are asked to remove our jackets from the back of our chairs because they were all akimbo, sleeves hanging on the floor. It's quite a comical scene as most of the tourists who have come to sample the famous *Sacher Torte mit Schlag* (chocolate cake with whipped cream) are American and very puzzled indeed by this request which seems so intrusive, so bizarre.

There are many rules in Vienna. Cleanliness, tidiness, is one of them. Specified forms of address according to status, another. It's confusing for an Austrian to address an emancipated American woman without a title, especially in a professional connection, and tempting for the American to make up a title so that she is taken seriously. Introducing oneself as "Carol Bergman" raises eyebrows here. The press officer at the Jewish Museum is "Dr. Stalzer." And answers the phone, crisply, with "Stalzer." His card says "Berater," consultant. Everyone in America is a consultant. What does this mean in Vienna?

Chloe comments that it must be difficult to be a young person here. Difficult to have fun. It's therefore surprising to find that the halls, staircases and open public spaces at the university are in a shambles, thick with smoke, graffitied, and derelict. The bathroom, which we desperately need to use after a morning of walking, are in utter disrepair, unusable in fact, worse than anything we have experienced in New York. This in contrast to the immaculate rest rooms we have found elsewhere in the city, with their floor to ceiling lockable doors, attendants, and perfumed towels.

My mother is disoriented. "Is that a skinhead?" she asks, pointing to a young woman at the photocopy machine with a shaved head and an odd scrambled swastika on her thick leather boots. In fact, we later learn, this woman is an anti-Nazi skinhead, her costume and the broken swastika a parody of the skinhead uniform.

Upstairs in the library there is a drunken man, as filthy and crazed as a bowery bum, lolling against the balustrade. The students seem oblivious; many are at computers, others are talking quietly.

"I don't remember the library to look like this," my mother says recoiling from the putrid, coffee stained walls. It doesn't seem as though anything has been cleaned up here for decades.

"Why would the students want to trash their own school?" Chloe asks, philosophically. "What are they trying to express here, that's what I'd like to know. I mean it's weird compared to the streets outside, isn't it?"

"Surreal. Like walking into a nightmare that won't quit," I say.

Steps, laboratories, wood-panelled rooms, all very much the same, all unrecognizable, my mother says.

We escape into the courtyard where there is fresh air and walk around slowly admiring the busts of famous scholars who made their reputations at the university. No Jews or women of note were honored in stone when my mother was a student here. Now we find the disembodied head of Dr. Julius Tandler, a Jew, who was my mother's anatomy professor and  Dr. Sigmund Freud who gave his first lecture on dreams in a small auditorium on the second floor.

"Still no women," Chloe says. "That says a lot."

We stop a young woman. Please, can you tell us what is happening here?

"I'm a graduate of the medical faculty," my mother says.

"I'm studying law. What would you like to know?"

She's a beautiful woman with long dark hair, dressed in an elegant bottle green pant suit. But her manner is haughty, and I'm sorry we've stopped her, and not someone else.

"*Schmutz*," my mother says. "The university is a slum."

The woman is shocked by my mother's directness.

"This university is free," she says. "Anyone in Austria can come here to study if they have the grades. It's what goes on in the classrooms that matters. There's no money for a custodial staff. It's a question of priorities."

"Then why don't the students take some paint and clean this place up, form a committee, get it done?," I ask. "What's preventing them from doing that?"

"We don't see the dirt," the woman says. "We're here to study, not to clean."

"Freedom," Chloe says as we skip down the steps back onto the Ring.

"Freedom?"

"It's some sort of expression of freedom."

"It looks more like anarchy and rage," I say.

"No. Inside the walls of the university, they are absolutely free," Chloe says.

*****

"I was born here. I was a Viennese," my mother says, tasting the words, savoring them.

She has been asked many times these past few days, "Are you or have you ever been a Viennese?"

Something she once was, central to her identity, but can no longer claim to be.

One night, after a Mozart concert, my mother feels hungry. Though it is late, the streets already deserted, we stop at a frankfurter kiosk to buy something for her to eat and drink. There are two men in Tyrolean suits drinking beer. They want to know *Gnädige Frau*, if my mother is or ever has been a Viennese. There is something different about her, the way she speaks, dresses, carries herself. And yet, there is something familiar about her, too.

One of the men is hanging back, the other is too close to my mother's back, hanging over her shoulder, drunk. I step in front of him, Chloe to one side, bodyguards.

I'm not certain if my mother is afraid, or even knows where she is.

Once upon a time she was a Viennese, she says, and then out flows the story of the Holocaust, and what she has left behind, what she has lost.

"I did not leave because I <u>wanted</u> to leave," she says, testing them. She has observed the gray Tyrolean jackets with green trim, the hats with feathers and pins, the dark brown corduroy trousers.

Costume of the Third Reich.

Others have gathered round. *Gnädige Frau*, apologies. Hitler made a terrible mistake asking you to leave.

"He did not <u>ask</u> exactly," my mother says, caustically, though she seems pleased that this dialogue is taking place. Since the confrontation in the Haslinger glove store, she has become more courageous and more relaxed. Not everyone is a Nazi. There is a new generation.

These men are not Viennese. They are visitors to Vienna, naïfs from the countryside who know nothing of *Schmäh*. Perhaps they're authentic. Perhaps what they say is truly how they feel. It's difficult to know, though we are now willing to give them the benefit of the doubt. This would not have been possible during the first days of our visit.

"This is my American daughter and granddaughter," my mother says proudly, introducing us. I'm grateful that this time she has left out the part about working for the American government. "We're here to ask questions and find answers."

"A pilgrimage," I add.

The man behind the counter smiles. He offers me a frankfurter, free of charge.

"I'm a vegetarian, thanks anyway," I say, my resistance slightly weakened by the pungent smell. Like the language, Austro-German food still nauseates and seduces me at the same time.

"Have you been to see the Monument Against War & Fascism?" my mother asks. "It will tell you everything you need to know. It's near the Opera. Walking distance from here."

Back at the hotel, a fax from America is waiting for us, greetings from my sister and her family. It's like a breath of fresh, crisp air after an oppressively hot summer day.

## CHAPTER 11: DEFINITIONS

Chloe wants to know, "What is it like to be a Jew in Vienna today?" But, for me, the question requires more precision. "What is it like to be a secular Jew in Vienna today? Or someone with a Jewish background who registers as *konfessionslos*, without religion? Is there discrimination? Is there still obsession with who is Jewish and who is not? Who is converted and who is not?

In his novel, Gebürtig, translated as "born of" or "native to," Austrian author Robert Schindel, the son of a survivor who returned to Vienna, weaves together the stories of two generations of Viennese Jews; survivors, their children, and the Gentile Austrians with whom they have co-mingled and intermarried for centuries. It was this secular culture that was wiped out during the Holocaust, along with orthodox Jewry.

Schindel's book has been a runaway best seller in both Austria and Germany and Schindel, previously known only as a poet, has been feted by the press in both countries.

"I'm a Jew in Vienna," he explained in an interview in The New York Times. "That's my country, my city. Less so Austria. That's a foreign country to me.... It is a fascinating city. The death wish, the humor, the anti-Semitism. Those anti-Semites don't even need Jews. They don't even know any Jews. If they did, they would be friends."

Schindel is on a book tour when we are in Vienna and will therefore not be able to meet with us. The press officer of the Jewish Museum, Dr. Alfred Stalzer (*konfessionslos*, born Catholic), suggests we talk to Annette Eisenberg instead. She is a recently appointed spokesperson for the City of Vienna, the American-born wife of Rabbi Chaim Eisenberg, the Chief Rabbi of Vienna. Stalzer says she will be able to answer Chloe's question: What is it like to be a Jew in Vienna today? But will she be able to answer my question about secular Judaism? Stalzer is oblivious to my concern that Annette is an orthodox Jew and encourages us to call her.

"I have never met a righteous Gentile," Annette says during our conversation in the cafe at the Jewish Museum. "They don't exist."

She is referring to the Gentiles who hid Jews during the war, helped them to escape, and risked their own lives. Annette Eisenberg doesn't believe they exist, a strange echo of Holocaust denial.

Worldwide, with variations on a theme depending on locale, ultra-orthodox Jews have an agenda, dictated by their fundamentalist beliefs. Ask a fundamentalist Jew if there still is antisemitism in Vienna or anywhere else and the answer will always be in the affirmative. There is a biblical source for this belief in the Book of Esther where it is written that the Lord offered the nations of the world the religious commandments which each rejected. When they were offered to the Jews, and accepted, hatred of Israel was simultaneously given to all the other nations.

It is the year of Schindler's List. And Schindel's book.

Annette has read Schindel's book, and liked it. Is this a spokesperson's diplomatic response or is it sincere? I'm not sure.

Wasn't Schindel saved by a Gentile family?

"Antisemitism is alive and well in Europe," Annette says. Whereupon she hands us a flyer she received from London printed by a right-wing group. It warns Gentiles that their children will be kidnapped by Jews and murdered during the Jewish festival of Purim.

According to Annette, there is no substantive difference between the primitive "blood libel" racism of the flyer and the discrimination she and her husband encountered when they were in the process of buying an apartment—the seller withdrew the contract when they found out they had a Jewish buyer. Did he know it was the Chief Rabbi of Vienna?

"Why didn't you sue the landlord for discrimination," I ask.

"There isn't any Civil Rights legislation in Austria," Annette says. "There are anti-discrimination clauses written into the Austrian constitution, but it is not the same. We would have had to sue. The burden of proof would have been on us."

I still wonder why such a prominent man, the Chief Rabbi of Vienna, decided not to expose this discrimination. It is odd.

Perhaps the fear of exposure?

My mother also fears exposure, fears "stirring things up."

Like Dorrith, Annette changes the subject. Would we enjoy a visit to the synagogue? She would be honored to give us a private tour. I have some questions about the museum, I say, hoping to return to the role of the orthodox community in today's Vienna.

I had read that the orthodox community objected to the Jewish Museum and delayed its opening for more than a decade. Why?

"We wanted the government to recognize the living Jewish community in Vienna today, not only give money for monuments to honor the dead," Annette explains.

But who are the dead? My family, other families in the Diaspora, some religious, some without religion.

And there's another important issue: the eagerness of progressive members of the Austrian government to face their complicity in the Nazi past by building monuments and funding museums, token gestures but important statements nonetheless. In my view, these gestures should be encouraged as there is a right wing resurgence in Austria. In the election of October, 1994, Jörg Haider's far right Freedom Party made significant gains. The party won 42 seats in the 183 seat legislature, making it the main opposition party. As of this writing in 1998, they still are sharing power. By contrast, the German far right Republican Party has no seats in the German parliament.

"Money is limited," continues Annette. "The Austrian government and the City of Vienna have an "unofficial" Jewish budget. No one admits it, but I feel it is a form of reparations. These moneys are fixed. Most of the community felt it was in their best interest to improve the inner structure of our living community before we improve our image in the eyes of the Austrian population."

I notice, with consternation, the omission of any mention of the secular Jews of Vienna before the war, now dead, or living in the Diaspora.

Correspondence with Dr. Kurt Schloz, adviser to Vienna's Mayor Zilk, contradicts Annette's assertion that money for projects proposed by the Jewish community were in any jeopardy whatsoever. On the contrary, the government seems to take the position that the Jewish community need just ask, and their wishes will be granted.

"I must admit, however, that I find it somewhat embarrassing to talk too much about the (material) support given to all these projects [the Jewish Old Age Home, Cultural Center, etc.]," writes Dr. Scholz in a letter to me on October 3, 1994, "because after the horrors of the Holocaust nobody will be able to make up for what happened—the events were much too terrible to allow for compensation by financial assistance."

\*\*\*\*\*

My mother is not enjoying our conversation with Annette Eisenberg. After the First World War, orthodox Jews flooded into Vienna from the East and her memories of their arrival are not pleasant ones. The newcomers were a reminder of an insular ghetto past. They spoke their own language (Yiddish), wore strange clothes, prayed as they walked along the street, and sent their children to special schools. They were easy to recognize as *Ausländer* (foreigners), unassimilable according to the antisemites, and an embarrassment to the educated, secular Jews in the professions who had risen above the ghetto into the upper middle class and beyond. My mother is still embarrassed by them and resentful that an orthodox rabbi now speaks for all Vienna's Jews, even the Reform Jews, who have their own synagogue, but are not "recognized" by the Austrian government.

It's getting late. Annette has a baby sitter waiting at home. She ends our conversation with an invitation to Friday services. We would be welcome. And there is a Hillel group in town visiting from Israel Chloe might enjoy, young people her age. Perhaps if we come, we will be able to meet her husband who will be conducting services.

But on Friday night, we have other plans, and they do not include prayer.

*****

When I traveled to Germany for the first time in the late 1960's, I had only a vague consciousness of being a Jew. My husband and I were invited by Dieter, a university friend, to Düsseldorf for a few days during the Easter holidays. In the international student counterculture of those years, barriers were easily transcended. It was before my awakening, the Holocaust still an unspoken hush.

I had heard that Düsseldorf had been decimated in the Allied bombing and was now a modern city entirely rebuilt with American money. There were jazz clubs and a cosmopolitan ambiance. But none of this, ultimately, mattered in Dieter's house. In between chitchat about toilet paper and what we would like for breakfast or dinner, were questions about my ethnic identity. His parents were curious: was I a Jew? I answered "yes," of course, not knowing what else to say, though there was a parallel question implied: What were you doing during the war? But I wasn't ready to ask it. Mostly, I was resentful that Germany and more particularly, these Germans, had the nerve to define me, solely, as a Jew, a word synonymous in Germany with "victim." The word Jew was an obstruction and they couldn't get past it. Nor could I when I was in Germany.

Involved in the Civil Rights struggle, the women's movement and, later, against the war in Vietnam, I defined myself—with political correctness appropriate to that era—as a white, middle-class, privileged American woman, among other things. In Dieter's house, it seemed, none of these categories meant very much with the exception of the word "privileged," as Dieter was a leftist, perhaps even a Marxist, eager to expound his theories on American Imperialism. Capital A. Capital I. We had long abstract political discussions late into the night. In the middle of one of these—I think it was three in the morning and we were chomping on some celery—it suddenly occurred to me that my grandparents, uncles, aunts and cousins had all been murdered just a few kilometers from Dieter's door. Unexpectedly, I felt frightened and told Jim I wanted to get out of Germany as soon as possible. We escaped to Paris where I could breathe freely again.

Now, in Vienna, so many years later, the visit to Dieter's house comes back to me and also my mother's facetious words during one of our tapings: "The Nazis made a good Jew out of me." She'd been so much more; a doctor, a Viennese, a European, an Internationalist, an art lover, a woman. Yet, when Hitler came, all that mattered was JEW.

We talk about our conversation with Annette late into the night. Chloe says, maybe we should wear a Star of David, just to see what happens. To see how we feel?

But, no, we are not believers, and a star has religious meaning. We met a skinhead the other night, drunk, flailing, he threw a beer bottle angrily at my mother's feet.

"If I'd been wearing a star I would have hidden it," Chloe says. We were afraid. JEW. VICTIM. We felt marked. Did he know?

Ridiculous, how could he have known? Why do you think Hitler forced the Jews to wear stars? Because no one could tell, unless you were an orthodox Jew; then it was obvious.

"Because of their geographical position, the Germans, just like the Austrians, are an especially varied people," writes German essayist Hans Magnus Enzensberger in an essay, "The Great Migration," published in <u>Granta</u> #42. "That blood-and-race ideologies gained credibility here of all places, can be understood as a kind of compensation to prop up an especially fragile identity."

## Chapter 12: Auf Wiedersehen (Good-bye)

My mother says she is leaving Vienna for the last time. She packs her bags the night before our departure and waits, sitting on her bed, unable to read. We have tickets to see Maximillian Schell in "My Fair Lady," but she doesn't have the energy to get dressed. "Imagine March 12, 1938 on CNN," I say, turning on the television in an attempt to get her moving.

As she is nervous and misplaces everything, I offer to carry her travel documents. She has watched me put them into my purse and then asks several times if they are safe, also if I'm certain that I've ordered the taxi for the correct time. Our plan is to take a train over the border into the Czech Republic and then to Theresienstadt, the Nazi death camp. My mother knows many people who died there.

Theresienstadt is not usually referred to as a death camp. The Nazis called it a "transit concentration camp." But this is, once again, a euphemism. All the concentration camps were death camps; prisoners were not sent there on holiday.

At breakfast, just an hour or so before we are to leave, my mother falls silent, her eyes clouded with memory.

"I don't think I'll have the strength to come here again with Joan next year," she says referring to plans my sister is making to repeat this journey with her family. "I'll have to explain, I'm leaving Vienna for the last time."

She picks at her food, has lost her appetite.

Checkout at the front desk and back to the room for our luggage.

Chloe says, "What about Fritzi? We've nearly forgotten about her during our stay here."

Minutes before our departure, the phone rings. It's Alexander Loebus, a student I've hired to do some archival research.

"Whatever is there you know already," he reports. "A run-down of her competitions. No personal information whatsoever."

*****

We have an African cab driver my mother doesn't trust. "He's taking a circuitous route," she says.

"What's the problem *Gnädige Frau*, don't you trust me?" the cabbie asks.

"Are you certain you know the way? Südbahnhof. The railroad station to the South."

"We are traveling South, *Gnädige Frau*," he says, and laughs, then draws deeper on his cigarette.

At the station, my mother is paralyzed and cannot move.

"Where are the porters? Where are my travel documents," she asks, nearly hysterical now, her arms flailing, her voice shrill.

We have arrived at the station with nearly an hour to spare because we know that getting up the escalator with our luggage will be difficult. Though there's a waiting room where we can read and rest, my mother decides to walk back and forth from one side of the inner courtyard of the station to the other.

Chloe and I agree, she is reliving her last moments in Vienna in the autumn of 1938. She and my father left from a train station much like this one on the other side of town, the Franz Josefs

Bahnhof, named after the Emperor.

Five young people with one suitcase each, false visas, a small amount of money. My mother was twenty-six -years old. My father, thirty-four.

One of my father's brothers had gold bullion stashed in the lining of his coat, another the family photographs, silver. My mother carried clothes, books and documents. Inside her long coat, too warm for a summer day, she trembled and shook. She held my father's hand. He put his arm around her shoulders. They tried to be cheerful. The situation was only temporary. Either the families would be reunited in Paris or they would be returning soon to Vienna when everything blew over.

Nanette and Berthold were there, also Helene and Adolf, my father's parents. On that day more than half a century ago, they hugged and kissed their children for the last time.

On the train into the Czech Republic, my mother is still unable to relax. There will be border guards and customs officials asking for our passports, searching our belongings. The clack of the wheels, normally so soothing in its dull monotony, becomes the racing heartbeat of a person on the run.

"The guards at the French border knew our visas were false," my mother says. "But they let us through anyway."

"We should have taken a plane," I say to Chloe quietly.

"We sit back and try to enjoy the passing landscape; green farmland, fields and fields of bright red poppies. We order three plates of salad and some Perrier from the club car and eat on small pull out tables.

The Austrian conductor who comes to collect our tickets is

friendly and wants to make certain my mother is comfortable. There has been a mix-up. Really we are supposed to be in a first class cabin, and he hopes everything is OK. He has some newspapers and magazines. Would we like them? He'll be disembarking at the border and wanted to say good-bye. We will notice a shift of personnel, different uniforms, the border guards. But the landscape will continue uninterrupted, the poppy fields sliced only by a thin barbed wire fence. What is a border anyway these days, he says, fast forwarding us out of the past into the present tense.

But when the border guards and customs officials knock on our cabin door, my mother is visibly alarmed. First the Austrians, unbelievably polite, and then the Czechs, a little more brusque, but very kind. They are interested in us, three generations of women traveling together. And only look cursorily at our passports. Americans, no problem, they say. And they do not even look into our bags or ask whether we have liquor or cigarettes or gifts.

My mother is transformed. "American passport. No problem," she says, and quickly finishes her salad which, by now, sits limply on her plate.

# PART III: THERESIENSTADT

## CHAPTER 13: ARNOLD

Once over the border into the Czech Republic, my mother is tracking Arnold's path into Theresienstadt, fifty kilometers northwest of Prague. The documents at the Kultusgemeinde in Vienna have revealed that Dr. Arnold Grätzer, Berthold's younger brother, and my mother's favorite uncle, did not die in Theresienstadt, as my mother had always thought, but in Auschwitz where he was transported from Theresienstadt on October 10, 1944. This was one of the very last transports to arrive in Auschwitz before the Allied advance.

By 1942, the Nazis had decided that slave labor and the Death Squads were not killing off Europe's remaining Jews fast enough. At the Wannsee conference, convened in a suburb outside Berlin by Deputy Reich Protector Heydrich, on January 20 of that year, the *Endlösung* (Final Solution), was again discussed and its progress reviewed. The Jews were tenacious and hardy. It was time to move faster. The whole of Europe must be *Judenfrei* (free of Jews).

After Wannsee, what had "hitherto been tentative, fragmentary and spasmodic was to become formal, comprehensive and efficient," writes Martin Gilbert in his book, The Holocaust.

Ten days later, on January 30, 1942, Hitler addressed a frenzied crowd at the Sports Palace in Berlin where he reiterated the resolution of the Wannsee conference. The speech, monitored by radio in London, included a by-now familiar sentence: *The war will not end as the Jews imagine it will, namely with the uprooting of Aryans, but the result of this war will be the complete annihilation of the Jews.*

This came as no surprise to anyone who had been listening to Hitler's speeches since 1939, or even before. And it certainly came as no surprise to anyone in the camps. By 1942, no one seriously believed that the troubles would "blow over." Nonetheless, the Wannsee Conference marked a turning point after which orders went out to accelerate the extermination of the Jews.

It is ironic, perhaps even criminal, that the American government refused visas for so many refugees in the early days of the war when Germany was still willing to grant exit visas to the Jews. "True, the Nazis wished to be rid of Jews," historian David Wyman has written in his book <u>Paper Walls: America and the Refugee Crisis, 1938-1941</u>, "but until 1941 this end was to be accomplished by emigration, not extermination. The shift to extermination came only after the emigration method had failed, a failure in large part due to lack of countries open to refugees."

"A deliberate policy of obstruction was under way, directed from the top of the State Department, from the man in charge of refugee matters, Breckenridge Long," writes Doris Kearns Goodwin in her book, <u>No Ordinary Time</u>. Eleanor Roosevelt prevailed upon her husband day after day to intervene, but he refused. "FDR, can't something be done?" she asked in one note to him. There is no evidence that he ever replied. Preoccupied with America's own preparations for war and the possibility of German annexation of Britain, FDR had no patience for any "sob stories."

\*\*\*\*\*

Arnold was deported to Theresienstadt seven months after

the Wannsee Conference. He lived in the camp for two years, working as a physician. His resourcefulness and intelligence was witnessed by Nanette's sister, Ida Sobotka, who survived Theresienstadt. "He kept many prisoners alive, including me," Ida had told my mother before she died of natural causes in a Viennese old age home in 1966.

Arnold looked so much like Berthold Ida had recognized him at once. And she was relieved to see him, of course. He had an authority and assurance that was comforting.

Ida's description of Arnold was familiar to my mother. She had known her Uncle Arnold as a sweet, loving unconventional man, a man who took risks. He was a second father to her during the four long years of the Great War when Berthold was a supply officer on the Russian front. Even after the war was over, Berthold was away a great deal, traveling into Yugoslavia to sell Haslinger gloves. But Arnold was around. A bachelor until 1926, he lived in the apartment at Josefinengasse #4 and set up a small office in the front room where he looked after the medical needs of members of the Viennese trolley union and their families. Like Berthold, Arnold was an active Social Democrat, (the progressive political party), and working for the union suited him; he was never interested in making a lot of money. Even after he got married, Arnold kept close contact with my mother and it was because of his encouragement that she decided to pursue her ambition of becoming a physician.

My mother doesn't know what happened to Arnold during the fallow period between 1938 and August 22, 1942, when he was deported to Theresienstadt. "He probably spent a lot of time in the cafe," she speculates, "talking politics and worrying about his wife and child, whom he had already sent away. And because he was my father's doctor, he might have stayed behind to look after him rather than organize his own escape. The two brothers were very close."

Arnold's daughter was eleven or twelve at the time of the annexation. Arnold, ever resourceful, had found a foster family for her in The Netherlands, but they gave her up to the Nazis after the invasion there in May of 1940, and she was killed.

Grete, his wife, had traveled to England, hoping Arnold would soon follow, but, by then, the borders tightly sealed, he couldn't get out. She eventually immigrated to America, but returned to Vienna and died there sometime in the 1960's.

These are the memories we are taking with us into Prague. Even here, it seems, we cannot be normal tourists enjoying the sights. History stalks us across the border, closing in on us as we approach the entrance to the camp.

## Chapter 14: Arbeit Macht Frei

"If it hadn't been for Arnold, I wouldn't have survived," Ida Sobotka had said.

I think of these words often as we enter the grounds of the Gestapo prison in the Little Fort in Theresienstadt.

We stand at the portal under the words *Arbeit Macht Frei* for a long time. I translate for Chloe, "Work will make you free," but have no idea what it means, even in English, though the phrase has become an icon of the Nazi era. Perhaps that is why it is so difficult to decipher, because it has lost its meaning or is so charged with association that we defend ourselves against interpretation.

Diana, whose father was murdered in Theresienstadt, is our guide here today. Though it's a hot summer day, she's wearing a black dress, as though in mourning. She waits silently while we gather. For a moment I imagine she is going to say a prayer and that we have, mistakenly, found ourselves in a house of worship. Or that we have been forcibly gathered and are awaiting interrogation, the men separated from the women, the children shunted to one side. Chloe and I are holding hands, unwilling to be separated, but my mother walks behind us, or in front of us, or to the side.

We're a group of twenty or so of varying ages: students from several European Union nations on a special fact finding mission; a couple, Rita and Ben, from The Netherlands; Ida, our guide from Prague; my mother, Chloe and me. Diana asks whether any of us have been to a death camp before. As it turns out, none of us has. The muscles in our necks are taut, our cameras cocked tight like the triggers of a gun.

What is my mother feeling?

"I know at least ten people who were in this camp," she says quietly.

Diana begins with the facts. "My dear friends, from November 24, 1941 when Theresienstadt was first opened until May 9, 1945 when it was liberated by the Red Army, 139, 654 prisoners passed through Theresienstadt."

Including Diana's father, Arnold Grätzer and Ida Sobotka. 207 children were born in Theresienstadt. Undoubtedly, Arnold attended some of the births. 701 prisoners escaped. Their fate is unknown. 33, 430 prisoners died either in the "Ghetto" itself a few kilometers down the road, or in the Little Fort.

The "Ghetto Theresienstadt" was formed in the the Czech town of Terezin where 10,000 people lived. They were all asked to leave and find accommodation elsewhere. After the war, many returned. Their descendants still live in the town today. Causes of death in both locations were the same: starvation, torture, disease, execution by gunfire. There is an execution wall a few feet from where are standing, bullet holes still starkly visible to the naked eye.

What can a doctor do in such a place? Staunch the flow of blood, put cold compresses on fevered foreheads, utter consoling words, keep himself from succumbing to starvation and disease so that he can continue to help others.

"If it hadn't been for Arnold, I wouldn't have survived," Ida had said.

These words become our mantra as we move from room to

room, cell block to cell block.

We are deadened, in order to survive this symbolic journey. Unable to cry, unable to laugh, unable even to ask questions when Diana asks if we have any.

"My dear friends," she says again and again, and then she tells a story about the daily lives of the prisoners, the atrocities, the heroism. Conditions in the "model ghetto," were in fact so horrendous, so foul, that it is difficult to comprehend how anyone survived at all. Survival, for any length of time in such a place, is a tribute to the tenacity of the prisoners, the ferocity of their will to live, their inner strength.

In this camp, deceptively portrayed to the world press as "a gift from the Führer to the Jewish people," Arnold found kindred spirits and collaborators against oppression. The prisoners here celebrated life, cherished it, developed survival strategies, arranged concerts, lectures and plays. The adults taught their children in makeshift schools, the young boys played soccer in opposing teams, artists held drawing classes, musicians tuned their voices or their violins. Unlike other camps, many of the prisoners in Theresienstadt were artists, actors, and musicians. This is why the Nazis dubbed it a "model ghetto." They used the camp to create an insidious propaganda film about what life was like for the Jews under German occupation. And they convinced a delegation from the International Red Cross that visited the camp on June 23, 1944 that the camp was an idyll where Jews were safe and happy.

"This was a very black mark in the history of the Red Cross," Diana tells us.

Death was a constant companion, always imminent, often a

relief from suffering. Dead bodies, no longer human, no longer named, were tossed like the bones of fish, into a state-of-the art crematorium, built by the prisoners themselves. Ashes from this crematorium were strewn into the Vltava river, so there would be no evidence. There were 17,472 alive bodies, or just barely alive, when the Red Army entered the camp. The Russians saved those they could save and buried the others in unmarked graves outside the walls of Little Fort. The rest, nearly 87,000, had been transported to the East to be gassed in death camps there, Arnold among them. Do these numbers add up? I really don't know. Nothing adds up when one contemplates genocide, tries to grasp it, tries to comprehend. How many died in Rwanda? How many in the former Yugoslavia where Berthold once traveled to sell gloves?

*****

9 p.m. back in Prague. We have had a rest, a Greek meal and are now sitting in the Church of St. Nicholas in the Old Town Square waiting for an organ concert to begin. Bach mostly, according to the program, healing melodies after our arduous day in the camp.

I take out pen and paper and begin to make notes. Chloe wants to write, too and so we begin an exchange:

*Carol: I keep seeing the blue straw flowers and the poppy flowers rolling by us in the fields, slowly, a slow motion film, and Ida, our guide, talking but no words coming out of her mouth. Passengers in the transport trains passed by these fields. Were there as many poppies and blue flowers fifty years ago?*

*Chloe: Whenever I imagine what it was like the scene is in black and white. Sometimes I forget color existed. I can only see gray. It must have been gray; color is too joyful, too alive, too horrific.*

*Carol: I see the poppies and the blue straw flowers. I feel the presence of everyone who died in Theresienstadt in this church. Baroque music—Bach, Handel, Telemann—is perfect tonight because the music is balanced and solid. An illusory permanence. The world is stable, it will not change, nothing terrible will ever happen again.*

*Chloe: I was scared in Theresienstadt.*

*Carol: You were very brave. You went into the chamber. Into it. I couldn't go.*

*Chloe: I knew I was being courageous. I couldn't stop playing with the film container box I was holding. But I didn't feel like crying, I felt like running.*

*Carol: Or killing?*

*Chloe: Running. And screaming at the top of my lungs: WAKE UP! like Spike Lee does in his movies. IT CAN'T BE TRUE. WHY DIDN'T THE WORLD WAKE UP? THEY WERE SYSTEMAT-IC. THEY HAD POWER. THE REST OF THE WORLD MUST HAVE BEEN ASLEEP. WAKE UP!*

My mother is sitting several rows in front of us, enjoying the music. Predictably, she was more angry than sad all day and unable or unwilling to cry. Now she wants to be alone again.

\*\*\*\*\*

Back at the hotel there's a jazz pianist playing Joplin in the cafe so we sit for a while and order some tea and apple strudel. The pianist makes us smile. He's having so much fun, his legs bouncing his long arms flying off the keys

"Freedom," Chloe says in a reprise of her observations about the students at the University of Vienna.

Prague is bursting with joie de vivre, music on very street corner, mostly jazz, the most fancy-free music of all.

"Can't wait to get on that plane tomorrow," my mother says. "What time do we have to get up? Have you ordered the taxi? Have you got my documents in a safe place?"

"Everything's done. Not to worry," I say. "In just a few hours you'll be home."

## EPILOGUE: A CONTINUING JOURNEY

I began this book with a search for a woman called Fritzi Burger, a member of my mother's family who emerged out of memory, then appeared, then disappeared again. But I haven't lost Fritzi as I feared I would when she withdrew her offer of a reunion in Maine or when the literal search for her dead-ended in the archives in Vienna. Or when I learned that she died in the spring of 1999 — on holiday in Austria — just as we were publishing this book. A person, and what the person has come to represent, cannot be lost if one continues to search, and then passes the search on to the next generation. Nor can she be entirely retrieved, either. The past — elusive, opaque, continually shifting in our memory — cannot ever be definitively retrieved, even by scholars and historians. It is the search that is important, particularly as we enter a new century and the survivors of the Holocaust, those with first-hand memories, pass on.

At first, I didn't understand that my search for Fritzi would primarily be a metaphoric one, that it would be a process of discovery, a journey. Like most journalists, I'm afflicted with a hunger to gather the facts, to establish corroboration, to record accurate quotes, to get to the bottom of things. I had thought I could recover memory, identity, and history in a finite way and that all my concrete questions of fact, sequence and provenance would be answered. After many months of searching, some have and some haven't. Depending on the letters I receive in the mail within the next year or two (because government bureaucracies are notoriously slow in Austria) I probably will be able to amend a fact or two in this book. I'll change a sentence here, a sentence there, add a footnote, delete another. I might learn more about Fritzi's father, for example, or the Haslinger glove factory, or what the Slunsky family was doing during the German annexation. I'll make a list of new questions that occur to me as the old ones are answered. I'll keep asking, probing, as will Chloe, and her children and her children's children.

Having said this—that the search is ongoing — I do think it's important to put the past to rest or at least to recalibrate it through the lens of our own individual perceptions and imperatives. Not to ever forget — that would be unconscionable — but to achieve some closure, and move forward out of the pain of the Nazi era and into the present where an ongoing dialogue with Austrians and Germans of parallel generations is essential, I feel, to achieve understanding, healing and permanent change. I know only a few survivors who are able to do this. I now feel that I can; certainly Chloe and her generation will. Embedded in their shared, electronic, transcontinental culture is the promise of world peace.

I think my mother feels closure, too, symbolized by the decision to pay for a gravestone in memory of Berthold and Nanette. It went up in December, 1994. Dorrith went out to the cemetery to take some pictures for us. When the photo arrived, my mother called to thank me and said, tearfully, she's glad it's there. And when we have discussions now about what we learned during our stay in Vienna, she seems to accept that there's a new generation of Austrians who are not all Nazis. On the contrary, many are the direct descendants of her father and uncle — Social Democrats — men and women with bold progressive voices. They, too, are part

of our lost (political) family. There is a volatile right wing opposing these voices, as there is throughout the western industrialized
world, including America. But the European Union vote was "Ja."
For the moment, therefore, I remain optimistic about the democratic future of both Germany and Austria, though I believe we
must remain vigilant.

On a personal note, my sweeping disdain and dread of <u>all</u>
Germans and <u>all</u> Austrians dissipated during the writing of this
book. This has been of great benefit and relief to me. After I
finished the first draft, I enrolled in a ten week German course at
NYU, a psychological challenge. After it was over, I decided not
to continue; it was too stressful. My teacher, who was born in
Stuttgart during the war, was very disappointed. I took her to
lunch and tried to explain, gave her a draft of this book to read,
and said goodbye. Months later, it is still hard for me to even small
talk in German to a waitress or a tourist. And I never speak
German to my mother or any of her Viennese friends. Though, of
course, I understand nearly everything.

I could have written about my father and his family, too, but
unfortunately he died in 1984 before I had the impulse to know.
And I am therefore grateful that my mother, throughout the process of gathering this book, has remained alert and strong. She has
also been very patient with me.

More than anything she has taught me this: that there are
many different ways of surviving the atrocities of a holocaust and
that we should not, must not, judge. My mother is one kind of
survivor, my cousin, Dorrith, another, my friend Isaak, another
still. Their circumstances were different, also their opportunities.

The malevolent forces that eracinated them from the past swept like a great storm washing over the coastline, transforming the contours of their lives forever. Yet, miraculously, they survived. More than survived, they built new lives, formed new attachments. My mother performed heroic deeds, kept her own zest for life intact. She has American children and grandchildren implying, despite Hitler's dire promises, new generations spiraling into the future without surcease. Dorrith does not, but she has us, her family in the Diaspora. In the end it all comes down to the same thing—after losing everything and everyone you have ever known and loved, you decide to go on living. This more than anything else, is what Dorrith, my mother, and so many other survivors, have in common. With this modest book, I hope I have honored them.

-END-

## WITH SPECIAL THANKS

In 1995, the world celebrated the 50th anniversary of the end of World War II. This book, however, was not quite finished and, even though my agent was hopeful, she could not sell it; the market was saturated. In the autumn of 1998, my mother turned 86 and though she is still healthy and dynamic, I decided it was time to self-publish. Fortunately, Jim and I had started a small desk-top publishing business and we knew how to put a manuscript into production. Still, we needed help. Enter the Bergman family. Our niece, Anne, a writer, editor and filmmaker living in Los Angeles, offered to copy-edit. What a joy to share so many e-mails. And Dale Voelker, her partner, who just happens to be a graphic designer (lucky me), offered to design the book. Jim became computer maven and managing editor, and Chloe, my profoundly talented artist-daughter, designed the cover. One small problem remained: to find a person to correct the German. Again, a relative of Jim's came to the rescue—the perspicacious Gerald Oppenheimer in Seattle. As a former librarian and a true scholar, not only did he make corrections, he did some extra historical research and guided me to a deeper understanding of the distinction between orthodox Judaism and fundamentalism.

To all of you, much love and thanks.

## ACKNOWLEDGEMENTS

*In New York:* Fredericka Zeitlhofer at the Austrian Cultural Institute, Dr. Gerline Manz-Christ and Sylvia Gardner-Wittgenstein at the Austrian Consulate. Rose and Isaak Arbus for reading the manuscript and continuing to ask questions. The Writers Group: Ann Baxter, poet, who was there at the beginning, Betsy Feist, Carol Skyrm, Jessica Jiji, Parul Kapur, Kris Williams, for sustenance and intelligence. Barbara and Fred Poll for good conversation, good food, and the loan of their library. Trude Poll for tracking down helpful people in Vienna and sharing her friend, Lucia. Harry Franklin, who we met serendipitously that day at the cemetery. Last, but not least, my dear husband and best friend, Jim, for his loving support, pep talks, incisive intelligence, and computer expertise.

*In Massachusetts:* Bibi Brown for her continuing interest and encouragement. After many years in hibernation, a retrieved friendship.

*In Seattle:* Gerald Oppenheimer, a survivor, for the cryptic note which got me started, and for his continuing offers of help over the years, always fulfilled. And to his wife, Millie, for her enthusiasm, interest and intelligent commentary.

*In Vienna:* Lucia Trautmann for the fax and her hospitality. Alexander Loebus for time spent in the archives. Dr. Alfred Stalzer at the Jewish Museum. Annette Eisenberg for her time and hospitality. Josef Kohut at the Central Cemetery for his patience and kindness. Dorrith. Words cannot express how it feels to know you.

*In London:* Norma Cohen for reading the manuscript, encouragement, wisdom and friendship everlasting. And Millie and Michael, too, with love and thanks for the space, mental and physical, to wind down after Vienna.

*In Prague:* Ida Hybnerova, a wonderful guide. And Diana, who held our hands in the Little Fort.

*In Holland:* Ben Carmiggelt and Rita Golstegn-Mers, for companionship during the tour of Theresienstadt, the photographs, the correspondence.

*In Poughkeepsie, Philadelphia, & New York:* My daughter, Chloe, for sharing the journey with me day-by-day, guiding me, and providing enlightenment and love. Infinity.

*In California:* Herb Cornell, for reading the manuscript with care and asking questions. Carol Tateishi, for her enthusiastic phone call which made my day, her friendship and encouragement.

*In Connecticut:* My mother, for the courage to tell her story. With love.

## SELECTED BIBLIOGRAPHY

Bellak, Leopold, *Confrontation in Vienna* (New York, 1993)

Beller, Steven, *Vienna and the Jews 1867-1938; A Cultural History* (Cambridge, 1989)

Berkley, George E., *Vienna and Its Jews; The Tragedy of Success 1880's-1980's* (Cambridge, 1988)

Clare, George, *Last Waltz in Vienna* (New York, 1980)

Dawidowicz, Lucy S., *The War Against the Jews 1933-1945* (New York, 1975)

Epstein, Helen, *Children of the Holocaust* (New York, 1979)

Gilbert, Martin, *The Holocaust; A History of the Jews in Europe During the Second World War* (New York, 1985)

Goodwin, Doris Kearns, *No Ordinary Time*, (New York, 1994)

Hoffman, Eva, *Lost in Translation* (New York, 1989)

Hofmann, Paul, *The Viennese; Splendor, Twilight and Exile* (New York, 1988)

Orgel, Doris, *The Devil in Vienna* (New York, 1978)

Pauley, Bruce, *From Prejudice to Persecution; A History of Austrian Anti-Semitism* (Chapel Hill, 1992)

Rosenbaum, Eli M., *Betrayal; The Untold Story of the Kurt Waldheim Investigation and Cover-Up* (New York, 1993)

Sartre, Jean Paul, *Anti-Semite and Jew* (New York, 1948)

Shirer, William, *The Rise and Fall of the Third Reich; A History of Nazi Germany* (New York, 1960)

Sichrovsky, *Peter, Strangers in Their Own Land; Young Jews in Germany and Austria Today* (New York, 1986)

Spitzer, Leo, *Lives in Between; Assimilation and Marginality in Austria, Brazil, West Africa 1780-1945* (Cambridge, 1989)

Wistrich, Robert, S., Antisemitism; *The Longest Hatred* (New York, 1991)

Wyman, David, Paper Walls: *America and the Refugee Crisis, 1938-1941* (New York, 1985)